SPRING 55

A JOURNAL OF

ARCHETYP

AND

CULTURE

GW00702274

Spring, 1994

SPRING JOURNAL
BOX 583
PUTNAM, CONNECTICUT 06260

ACKNOWLEDGMENTS

To Princeton University Press for quotations from the *Collected Works (CW)* of C. G. Jung (Bollingen Series XX), translated by R. F. C. Hull, edited by H. Read, M. Fordham, G. Adler, and Wm. McGuire, and published in Great Britain by Routledge and Kegan Paul, London. Other quotations have been acknowledged throughout in appropriate notes and references.

Spring is printed in the United States of America, text on acid free paper.

Spring is the oldest Jungian journal in the world. It was founded in 1941 by the Analytical Psychology Club of New York. In 1970, James Hillman transferred its editing and publication to Zürich, Switzerland. From 1978 to 1988, it was edited in Dallas, Texas. Since 1988 it has been edited in Connecticut.

CONTENTS

SPRING 55: THE ISSUE FROM HELL

I n trying to illustrate the theme of this issue with an appropriate cover, we settled on a photograph of the old and abandoned, graffiti-strewn but still majestic Worcester, Massachusetts train station as it looks today. It was through those grand portals and down those dilapidated steps that Freud and Jung once descended together, no doubt with some anxiety even for them, at the climax of their famous trip to the United States in 1909. They had come to Worcester to receive honorary degrees (their first) from Clark University. Worcester, and America, too, for that matter, looked a lot more blueberry beautiful then than it does now, but these two Masters of the (psychological) Universe nonetheless pronounced the land (in their later memoirs) as certifiably dark and diabolical. Freud's bowels were bothering him and Jung wasn't happy until he could make camp in the Adirondack mountains. Hell, after all, is where you find it.

Some might take the old train station as an image of urban America itself these days. But that's not our view at all. As the Dallas Institute for the Humanities has long maintained, American cities, for all their horrors and grizzly thrills, are often at their most soulful in the worst neighborhoods.

We think Worcester is a delightful place even today, not because we're relativists at the *Spring Journal* (who think Hell is in the eye of the beholder), but because we're archetypalists. We see Hell (and a lot of other subjects) as a long-term proposition that won't go away.

Perhaps we know too many depressed people for whom life is hell (and too many depressing people who make it hell) to deny its existence altogether. So articulating its contemporary nuances and checking out its latest architecture is a task that *Spring* undertakes with gusto.

Hell is found in places you don't expect. And we think we've come up with a few surprises in this issue. Michael Perlman, a writer in the burgeoning new field of eco-psychology, finds hell in the psychological torment that afflicted people after Hurricanes Hugo and Andrew, especially as they reflected on "hurt" trees. Noah Pikes, a voice teacher, hears the sounds of hell repressed in the human voice and argues for their release. Greg Mogenson, a psychotherapist, finds hell in domestic atrocities. If you thought math was hell when you were in school, Robert Early, a mathematician, is sympathetic, although he finds soul there, too. Stephen Karcher, an expert in the Chinese divination technique of the *Yi Ching*, ponders the devils and demons lurking in Judaeo-Christian (and Western science's) hostility to the practice of divination. And psychologist Richard Noll reminds us of Jung's most hellish personal fear, the theory of degeneracy propagated by Max Nordau.

This is a fiendish brew, as the late Vincent Price might say. And to spike it even more, we've tossed into the pot a new feature for the journal: Letters to the Editor. Our readers apparently like to give us hell, so it seems appropriate to share some of their spleen with you. We include in our Jungiana section a different if no less intriguing correspondence, the letters between Richard Hull and Michael Fordham, the translator and editor of Jung's *Collected Works* for the English-speaking world. Their letters are eye-opening documents for anyone who still thinks Jung's texts (at least their English translations) were, like the Worcester train station, carved in granite.

You may not find *The Issue from Hell* altogether pleasant reading. But think of it as the next best thing to being there.

The Editors

TREES OF PAIN AND DEATH

MICHAEL PERLMAN

I. Gatherers of Pain

T rees clearly suffer. As Gaston Bachelard says, "The suffering tree is the epitome of universal pain."[1] While we register—in part spontaneously and involuntarily—the tree's own sensitivity to its surroundings, we understand this as an active power of the tree. We become sensitive to the psychological presence of trees. But this sensitivity can also register in us as the experience of difference between trees and ourselves.

When I first drove northeast out of Charleston on Highway 17, I went straight into this pain. Highway 17 cuts through the eastern edge of the Francis Marion, in the area hit hardest by Hurricane Hugo's 140mph-plus winds. The hurricane made landfall over Charleston itself, but the most intense part of the storm, its northeastern quadrant, passed over the Francis Marion. As I continued northward, low clouds and fog that had shrouded the landscape burned off, and the sun revealed a desolate scene. Many ruined buildings were still boarded up, though I saw several people emerge from small wretched houses. For miles on either side of the highway, the forest, mostly pine, was

This article is excerpted from the author's book, *The Power of Trees: The Reforesting of the Soul,* forthcoming from Spring Publications. The people interviewed in the article live in areas devastated by Hurricane Hugo in 1989 (South Carolina), and Hurricane Andrew in 1992 (South Florida).

flattened. A few tall, scraggly trees remained, most with few limbs or needles and bent toward the southwest, away from the hurricane wind. All other forest trees (the loblolly pines) over about twenty feet tall were either snapped off or uprooted, with the trunks and limbs falling in the same direction. In the hardest hit communities on or near the coast, like Awendaw and Mc-Clellanville, oaks and other hardwoods stood without limbs, or with half of their crown dangling and dead; others lay sprawled, having pulled up huge clods of earth as they fell over.

There was sun where shade and shadow should be. I passed a field of broken trees on my right where the ground had been blackened by fire. Men in heavy work clothes were gathering piles of limbs together and burning them. White smoke wafted over the highway. I felt faintly nauseous. I understood now what Susan, a secretary with whom I had spoken by phone had told me. When she got up the morning after the storm and looked out at the downed trees, "It just made me sick to my stomach. I felt on the verge of going into shock." Dangling, twisted limbs in too much sun assaulted me on all sides. Various images of war—from Vietnam and of the leveled cities of Hiroshima and Nagasaki—came to mind: Images of rubble, of dead trees, of blast-bent smokestacks. The tangled limbs and branches—"rough," in foresters' parlance—especially reminded me of bombed-out ruins—even of human remains. These, and more general images of a polluted industrial wasteland somehow merged in my overall impression of miles of tree trunks snapped off at between fifteen and twenty feet from the ground. It still disturbs me, this image of a blasted forest of smokestacks.

Susan's home is in the Francis Marion. In her mother's yard was a white flowering dogwood tree that had been blown over by the storm. Since this tree still had roots in the ground and was small enough to be handled, Susan propped it back up and tried to reroot it. As she said when we met, "It was nice to be able to...save something like that. Or even try." A friendly, worn-looking woman in her thirties, Susan was reluctant to voice her emotions directly. When I asked how she felt just after she had propped the tree back up, she hedged: "You really didn't have time to think about it." But then she responded with an image: "When that tree...flowers out [in the spring], I'll feel a lot of satisfaction." I asked how she might feel then, standing by the tree while it is flowering, and Susan replied, "I'd probably want to hug it or something."

Her spirit flowed kinaesthetically into the righted tree, and its spirit into her. But, though the image was one of hope and beauty, it also evoked deep pain, which I felt at the moment as a sudden wave of sadness. It seemed that Susan was about to cry, but she stopped herself: "Well—sometimes it doesn't pay too much to think about all this stuff, you know? You can't really concentrate on...a few single things too much, because you'll be disappointed, maybe, you know?"

The commingling of beauty and pain is not unique to Susan. Trees can elicit tears, as they did in David. And we can compare the sequence of David's narrative to Susan's image; each amplifies the other. In David's case, helpers arrived to right his three palms. "And they stood 'em up for me. Started cryin'. I couldn't help it...it was pretty to see 'em come up...those guys helped put me on the track...because a tree's comin' up, all the sudden we're goin' again." In each case, it is the *righting* of the tree, combined with a prospect of beauty, that releases pain. The human-tree analogy becomes emotionally and kinaesthetically embodied; Susan and David get in touch with a human grief—but equally they are in touch with something nonhuman—or are momentarily transformed into tree spirits.

We can learn from this about "The Ecology of Grief," to use the title of an article by Phyllis Windle, a plant ecologist and hospital chaplain. Windle notes her own response to reading that a blight could annihilate dogwood trees. This "stunned" her. "Memories of dogwoods came flooding back....I remember my first wild dogwoods. Across a southern Illinois field, a few gloriously white-blooming trees stood against a backdrop of dark pines. I was doing field work with the man I loved, and those wild trees blossomed in my heart, too."[2] She realizes that "I am in mourning for these beautiful trees." She reflects on environmental scientists' deep love for "their organisms," and how in a time of massive species loss this poses particular difficulties. "Notice how quickly developers accuse us of caring more for spotted owls, snail darters, and wildflowers than for people. Our guilty backpedaling suggests we know they are right, at least about our love for the organisms and places in which we invest our life's work, if not about how people rank in our affections."

Remember that Will complained that some people in the Earth First! movement seemed to care more about trees than human beings. But then he, too, was susceptible to the love of dogwoods. As the experiences of David and Susan suggest, one need not have invested one's life work in ecology in order to feel deep grief over ecological loss.

What also makes it hard, whether one is a biological scientist or not, is that societal assumptions "may make environmental losses difficult to grieve. We have almost no social support for expressing this grief." Indeed, one staff member at Fairchild Tropical Garden said that "a lot of us were ashamed to admit how depressed we were" over what Hurricane Andrew did, as though such grief were somehow inappropriate.

Frank, a South Florida botanist, struggled not to cry as he reassured me (and himself) that nature would "come back." But he couldn't contain his tears when thinking of the remaining trees coming back into leaf and flower—like freshly unfolding pain. He seemed profoundly uncomfortable about being so emotional about what his training told him would renew itself; but the logic of his loving attachment to what he wanly referred to as "my life's work" follows a different grain. In Frank's case, his botanical knowledge made mourning harder. It was an ecological image that made it nonetheless possible—the releafing of the trees, the spirits in the leaves.

Fortunately, Dan, the South Carolina forester, worked in a setting where there was support for grieving. He became tearful the moment we sat down to talk. A tall, bearded man, Dan recalled driving back through the forest with his wife and children, after having taken shelter from Hugo in the western part of the state:

> "When I got into the national forest and saw the areas, the stands that I was familiar with and worked in—well, I just cried. 'Cause it was just devastating to see this 100-year-old longleaf [pine] just laid flat just as far as the eye could see...I really did have to just pull off the road for a minute, it affected me so much I...just couldn't continue drivin'. And everybody I met those first few days was like that—it gets me choked up to start thinkin' about it...I'd gotten to a point where I'd adjusted to the idea [but during] the first few weeks [when] I'd have to drive right back through the forest and look at all of it, I'd find myself cryin'...But everybody I talked to, the guys that work on the forest, the timber markers, the guys like that—these rough, tough guys—they all had tears in their eyes. They loved this forest—as I did."

Pamela, who didn't work in such a congenial setting (a car rental agency), seemed to say obliquely that the destruction made her want to cry when she remembered walking in the woods as a child: "What gets me about the trees is that—I actually used to start to cry when I saw the sun shining through the trees, like on summer days or spring days...just seeing the sun shine." In each case, the words of a curator of an English botanical garden after the October 1987 storm apply: "I can think of nothing so heartbreaking for a gardener that [sic] to sit indoors and hear the sound of trees going over one by one."[3]

One of the first things we learn from Trees of Pain is that our grief over ecological loss has to be taken on its own terms, and that the general lack of acknowledgement of such grief in our culture may cost us dearly. In our era of global ecological concern, it is worth taking seriously what Dan says of the destruction of the forest: It "is almost like a death in the family, it's the same kind of feeling. It takes the same period of time and all to work your way through it, it's not somethin' that you can get over in a week or somethin'." Or when Steve likens the destruction of Fairchild Tropical Garden to "hearing that someone you were really close to died, because it's sort of like a living organism—everything's alive here." That's why, on the morning after Hurricane Andrew, Steve and his girlfriend, on seeing "sticks and no order...got choked up and started to cry". He called this "just like an instinctive reaction; it was like an overwhelming loss." Trees of Pain tell us we love far more than we know.

Because we love far more than we know, we do not grasp the full power of trees in regard to pain, the far-reaching "ecology of grief," if we go no further than to say that people can cry or feel genuinely heartbroken over the loss of trees that, in Susan's words, "you get attached to." For there are times "when loss leans like a broken tree," and that trees, broken or not, have the power to evoke unexpected depths and reaches of loss in us.[4] They have the power to evoke the felt images of brokenness, in all their forms. In Susan's case, her imaginative contact with the dogwood tree evoked the whole of the loss she felt in connection with the hurricane, including prior family losses. For Dan, the devastation of the forest was also an uprooting of his family's deep attachment to their home since the Revolutionary War—and it intensified his sense of dislocation in the human and bureaucratic world. Pamela keenly felt a basic loss of her early connections with nature.

Jane started to cry when she related her favorite old apple tree, with its "accumulation of pain," to the depth of estrangement she perceives between human and nonhuman life (trees, she said, are like "strangers in a strange land"). Afterwards, she added that the "tree knows there's a threat" to the ecological future. That is, the imaginal power of the tree brings to awareness the threat Jane feels and knows. The power of trees evokes a heightened awareness of pain, and the knowledge that comes from such awareness. This is not a new insight; after all, the author of Genesis 2 knew that trees of knowledge can be trees of pain.

Particularly revealing of the reach of Trees of Pain is the way Lewis, the Homestead plant physiologist, juxtaposed his response to the trees hurt by Andrew with a more personal wound—his recent divorce. Lewis, a boyish-looking thirty-one, described how he had begun to try to reconstruct his life after the divorce, when "here comes this hurricane. And I was *just* getting things started and *WHAM!* it's all wiped clean," he said. "It's so amazing—the thing that really upset me, almost more than anything," was the loss of a particular grapefruit tree he had recently planted. This is what led Lewis to angry words with Andrew: "'You could have wiped out everything, but maybe you coulda left me that one tree.'...it just means I have to start over again. And I've been startin' over again too much," he said, with a tense laugh. Lewis recognized something important in his attachment to "that one tree," the way "it just symbolizes," as he put it, the way his life is back on hold. The felling of the tree *brought up* in a very immediate way Lewis's frustration at the thwarting of his life goals—the growth of "my tree."

Lewis insisted that the native trees of the area can "handle" hurricanes. But "it was devastating to me to see everything just missing leaves." Immediately—like David and Susan—he imagined recovery: "Now one of the therapeutic things was when you actually started digging through your trees, and you could lift up a tree, and underneath it there'd actually be a small tree that had made it because of the big one [that] fell on it." And "a few leaves make you feel so much better" because "they hide the damage...the jags and the metal." As with David and Susan, the image of tree recovery serves to quicken pain: "First thing I did was get all the metal out of the trees, 'cause that was the real [disturbing thing]...I'd see that metal in the tree and that—that really affected me. *Didn't* like it. It, uh, I don't know what it made me feel, it just made me think of destruction." For "twisted metal" in leafless, broken trees "just makes you feel *so* horri-ble..."

Like David and Susan, Lewis then imagines vertically: "Even when a tree's laying on its side, you get it set up and you feel better 'cause at least then you've tried to do somethin' and the tree then has a chance." Lewis, like David and Susan, struggles for a kind of efficacy, for doing something—in an arboreal way. The tree is upright and, kinaesthetically, that also gives the hu-man self a chance at new vitality. But once again pain also gets new vitality.

Lewis next spoke about his first trip out of the Homestead area after Andrew. As he drove northward, looking at the destruc-tion, "I started to cry—which is interesting," he added, perhaps in part to keep a handle on his emotions right then. After he had driven beyond the area of greatest damage, he found himself real-izing how important it was to again see leaves on the trees. "I thought to myself, This is *Paradise*, compared to where I just came from." Then more grief begins to leaf out: "It was interest-ing because I hadn't really been e—emotional" about the storm before. His subsequent struggle for words was painful to listen to: "And still, though, the hurricane emotions on my indel-ible—I mean, on my, uh, unevenness about my emotionalness, you know, or getting—getting emotional about things—I know this hurricane will not affect me as much as my divorce. I *still* get emotional about my divorce, *constantly*. You know, I'll be—I'll be just driving home, and suddenly I'll get hit with it." Of course, the hurricane and the divorce are psychologically very much connected and intensify each other; Lewis's grief over his divorce makes "the hurricane emotions" more difficult—but in their own way, those also are "indelible." Both are heightened by trees.

Lewis's predicament, and his personal psychological style, dif-fer from David's and Susan's, but the way in which trees reach complexities of pain is remarkably similar in all three. It is the precise joining of broken trees and "hope for a tree," to use the words of Job (14:7), which joins human and nonhuman loss. The felt pain is the resurgent power of the trees' bodily spirits.

In poetic and literary settings, too, trees can heighten pain. Consider another image of natural destruction, this one from a poem by Mary Oliver called "Rain": "All afternoon it rained, then [the lightning] as authoritative as God is supposed to be," struck. "When it hit the tree, her body/opened forever."[5] That opening quickly ramifies. The poem next depicts men trying to escape on a rainy night from a detention camp, climbing a barbed-wire fence. "In the darkness...handful after handful of barbed wire." And again, in the rain, the narrator sees death, in the form of her uncle after his suicide. In the poem's history, "natural" violence to a tree, rendered with sensual and nonhuman detail, is juxtaposed with human violence and loss, so that they speak to each other.

Trees need not be utterly devastated in order to evoke shared pain and social concern. When Miss Amelia and her hunchback Cousin Lymon, the principal characters in Carson McCullers's short novel, *The Ballad of the Sad Café*, go upstairs to bed after their first meal together, the lamp Miss Amelia holds "made on the staircase wall one great, twisted shadow of the two of them."[6] This is McCullers's way of illuminating and foreshadowing the twists and deformities of love and of morality in the South that is the subject of this and her other work. Miss Amelia and Cousin Lymon are very much at one, it turns out, in their mingled capacities for love and for ruthless exploitation of one who loves them. Miss Amelia first brutally spurns a man's love for her and then milks him for everything he's got during a marriage that lasts ten days. However, she loves Cousin Lymon. But Cousin Lymon doesn't return her love. Instead, he exploits Miss Amelia's love for him and eventually participates in her ex-husband's revenge against her. The story is about "one great, twisted shadow" of love.

There are other shadows in the story. As Cousin Lymon first arrives one evening, "The moon made dim, twisted shadows of

the blossoming peach trees along the side of the road." Intro-
duced in the first sentence of the novel, the peach trees mirror
the course of the narrative. Their blossoming, "light as March
clouds," is coincident with Miss Amelia's first flush of love for
Lymon: her love *is* that beautiful, and her character mirrors the
complexities of the peach trees themselves. The café that flourishes for a time, and inspires a sense of community heretofore
lacking among the townspeople, is also like the trees. At the
time of Miss Amelia's marriage, over a decade before the arrival
of Cousin Lymon, "the peach trees...were more crooked and
smaller" than when the café flourished. But now, years after the
tragic denouement, mirroring the decaying town and a now aged
Miss Amelia, "The peach trees seem to grow more crooked
every summer, and the leaves," seen in the merciless August sun,
"are dull gray and of a sickly delicacy." They portray the bro-
ken-down spirit of the place. Imagistically, these sickly trees can
be compared to the "stunted, smoke-blackened tree" with "new
leaves of a bilious green" that anticipates the tragic denouement
of McCullers's novel, *The Heart is a Lonely Hunter*.[7] The stunted,
stifled peach trees configure Miss Amelia's biography and the
history of a mythic town—the suffering and decay (and also the
tenacious life) in the rural American South which McCullers's
fiction probes.

A still starker illustration of the power of trees to evoke social
pain is a particular chokecherry tree that grows on the back of
Sethe, the former slave woman and protagonist of Toni Morrison's *Beloved*.[8] You don't see the tree at first, and Sethe herself
doesn't know it is there until, fleeing slavery after being gang-
raped and then brutally beaten, and now about to have a baby,
the tree is discovered by a white girl who finds Sethe in the
woods and briefly cares for her. The girl unfastens the back of
Sethe's dress and describes the wound:

> It's a tree...A chokecherry tree. See, here's the trunk—it's red
> and split wide open, full of sap, and this here's the parting for

the branches. You got a mighty lot of branches. Leaves, too, look like, and dern if these ain't blossoms. Tiny little cherry blossoms, just as white. Your back got a whole tree on it. In bloom. What God have in mind, I wonder. I had me some whippings, but I don't remember nothing like this. Mr. Buddy had a right evil hand too. Whip you for looking at him straight...Whoever planted that tree beat Mr. Buddy by a mile.

Morrison reverses the conventional association of trees with flourishing life, so that planting a tree embodies flourishing pain and oppression. But these grimmer embodiments are as ancient as are trees of life; and the chokecherry tree in American lore is often unwanted, a weed tree. At the same time, though, Sethe loves trees. Even where she had been enslaved, there were "the most beautiful sycamores in the world...Try as she might to make it otherwise, the sycamores beat out [her two runaway] children every time and she could not forgive her memory for that." She treasures the woods that shelter a clearing in which her mother-in-law would preach, that "green blessed place" where "woods rang" when the assembled sang. And Sethe is about to give birth—another way of planting a tree—to a daughter who at one point sleeps outside so that, "She smelled like bark in the day and leaves at night..." (Sethe's tree-daughter would appear to take after an image of Janie Crawford's mother in Zora Neale Hurston's *Their Eyes Were Watching God.* Janie's grandmother, during her escape from slavery at the conclusion of the Civil War, at one point "wrapped Leafy," as she called her newborn daughter, "up in moss and fixed her good in a tree" until sure that "all of us slaves was free.")[9] Part of what makes for Sethe's pain, after being discovered by the white girl and later on when she is caressed by her lover, is what brought whelming sadness to Susan, Dan, Jane, Pamela, and Lewis. In the white girl's words, "Anything dead coming back to life hurts." The way trees gather pain is the way they raise the lost and the dead into new life but also configure irrevocable wounds. Loss lives in trees. That is why Sethe, years later, began to cry when her lover "rubbed his cheek on her back and learned that way her sorrow, the roots of it; its wide trunk and intricate branches."

II. Trees of Death

Not only can the dead come to life in trees, but the living can go to death. This may take an oblique form, as in Annie Dillard's images of Beal Obenchain as a *piling driven into sand,* and of a local Indian fatally wounded—a "stake had been driven into the ground, and he had been driven onto the stake."[10] The stake had been driven deeply into the ground, and the man rooted there, as it were, like the "Rooted Woman" of Kwakiutl mythology who inhabits the house of Man Eater; or, in another way, like Christ on the *tree* of the cross.

Trees can not only evoke pain but *secure* life's connections with death. Death's images are inherent in the memory of woods. Listen again to Mary Oliver's poem, "Rain": "under the trees/the black snake/jellies forward" and rubs against "little boulders of bark,/to take off/the old life." He knows:

> these are the woods of death,
> these are the woods of hardship
> where you crawl and crawl,
> where you live in the husks of trees,
> where you lie on the wild twigs
> and they cannot bear your weight,
> where life has no purpose
> and is neither civil nor intelligent.

All our persisting fantasies of "dark woods" indicate how death flourishes snakelike among the trees. Think again of Will's Old Folk Trees, and the ranks of Trees of Fear. Think of certain yew trees Sally recalled, which grew outside of her parents' kitchen, "very dark"; nothing could grow beneath them; and when you went out there you noticed a "strange smell." Their "kingdom" had a kind of "sinister" quality that "sort of sucked you in." And "the tree trunks were strange"; they "had [a] sort of flaking bark which, if you rubbed against, you'd get green..." The trees deposited a thick carpet of needles, "and you'd get the kind of strange feeling that things were buried there, and you didn't quite know what it was." What might these things have been? I asked. Sally replied, with a slight gasp, "It could've been cats." Then she added: "I never felt bodies. And I tended not to dwell on those sorts of things anyway."

Yew trees, in part due to their dark quality, have legendary associations with death and cemeteries.[11] But death among trees is far more pervasive than that. The Kwakiutl forest was also a cemetery. The woods may evoke involuntary anticipations of death. Will imagined the wooded hills of his childhood home that way. And David Rains Wallace writes about nearly getting lost in a Florida woodland, when he noticed a large orb weaver spider that "had caught a young anole lizard in its web, had wrapped it in silk, and was eating the flesh of its head. The lizard's white skull gleamed strangely from the gray web."[12] Shortly thereafter, "I saw myself lying beneath a fallen branch, my skull gleaming like the anole's." Wallace's own mortality gleams whitely in this vision of woods as *the web of death*. We find another such figuration in a story about soldiers on patrol in Vietnam mountains during the war—in the "Jungle, sort of, except it's way up in the clouds and there's always this fog...everything's all wet and swirly and tangled up and you don't see jack, you can't even find your own pecker to piss with. Like you don't even have a body."[13]

There are no limits to ways in which trees can prompt an encounter with deaths. Every tree grows posthumously.

Sally was fifteen when her mother died. She remembered, "I was asked if I wanted to go in and see her body. And I chose not to, because it was too painful." But her still incomplete mourning (she "didn't...so openly explore" her pain at the time of her mother's death) was re-evoked when Sally spoke of her deeply felt horror "when you see, like on television...one of these giant forest trees in the Amazon or something just being felled...crashing down and destroying stuff below and all the life above...all these trees could be crying out in unison and most people do not...hear..." Sally did hear "the sound of the forest, the sound of the cry and the crash, [and] the silence afterwards," adding that this "silence after the destruction of the forest that has gone on forever—as we know it—is quite horrifying, you know?" When I asked if she could recall any other times when she felt such horror, Sally paused. Her response showed what else the television tree spirits could say:

> Well, in a strange way—I suddenly got this thought that it re- lated to the way that I felt when my mother died. That there was a lot of activity in our home, there was a lot of life in our home. There were people coming and going. There was nour- ishment and nurturing...and life that just...revolved around her, and out from her. And when she died—and I have this very very strong image that I'll probably carry to my grave—the door to her bedroom was closed (and I didn't go through because I didn't want to see her dead). That door shut on that life there. And there was a palpable silence about the way the life revolved within the house after that, or...it was cutting off the mother...it was the silence of death. And I be- lieve that's what the silence is when they cut the great trees down in the forest.

The trees, Sally's mother's life, and something in Sally and in her family's life are in their mirroring way cut off and cut down.

Trees hold together death and survival. The uncanniness of trees of death has to do with the way death not only ends life but survives in it. Life grows on death, and death grows on life. The multifarious traditions linking death, burial, and trees re- flect this awareness. They show love but also the persistence of death. Jan, a young woman, described the funeral service for her mother, who had died recently. She was cremated and, at Jan's suggestion, the family buried her ashes under a tree in the family small cemetery plot. But if her ashes were buried under the tree, Jan reasoned, the tree would take them up and make them part of its life. To Jan's surprise, her whole family embraced this idea. Her father, whom she thought would not be receptive, added that he would like his ashes placed beside his wife's. There is a memorializing and witnessing of human life here, but not exactly an immortalizing of it. In a contemporary rural Greek lament, the author wonders: "My beautiful cypress tree, where would you like me to plant you?" and then resolves: "I will plant you in the graveyard,/so that you can spread out your boughs and branches."[14] Death lives in trees, where it becomes the heartwood of survival.

It is in part because every tree has roots in the posthumous that it can be particularly important for people to know that trees will survive them or their loved ones. That importance is also apparent in the response of people to the sudden loss of trees. That evil wizard whom Treebeard let out made his way to the hobbits' homeland, the Shire, where at his "bidding [trees] had been cut down recklessly far and wide"; Sam, one of the main hobbit protagonists, "grieved over this more than anything else. For one thing, this hurt would take long to heal, and only his great-grandchildren, he thought, would see the Shire as it ought to be."[15]

Just about everybody I talked with after Hugo and Andrew pondered the *lasting* quality of the destruction of trees. In South Carolina, people's responses were typified by the first Charleston newspaper editorial after the hurricane: "Never in our lifetime will the city of Charleston look the same. Neither will much of the surrounding Lowcountry..."[16] Pamela told me with wistful sadness that "it will *never* grow back again—not the way it was." Especially painful for many was a sense of shared, *generational* loss. Said Dave, the wildlife biologist: "Our generation will never see it the same..." Dan, the forester in the Francis Marion, spoke for many, in the Lowcountry and South Dade

County, when he said, "You don't realize that people who live through things like this have to live with it for years..." Ted observed with quiet frustration, "Houses can be rebuilt...but you can't rebuild a forest. It will not be back the same in our lifetime." Kevin, summarizing what many residents in the Charleston area told him about the loss of trees in their yards, said they would have preferred that houses and not trees be gone when they returned after the storm: Houses can be fixed. "But they will never live to see the trees in the same condition they were in. There just is not enough time left in their lives to have...sixty-foot pines back in their yard, or oaks..."

For some people around Homestead, the trees had receded into the background of concern. Frank, for instance, reversed Ted's statement, saying, "You can grow trees but you can't grow houses." Reconstruction had been agonizingly slow, and the less-tangible but no less traumatic psychological effects of the storm were taking their toll. And for three months it had been, as one woman made homeless by the storm put it, "hot and stinky." Yet, as Frank's remark suggests, the trees were still psychologically present—or absent, despite new greening. Despite the difference between Frank's and Ted's responses, both evoke the connection between trees, houses, and shelter. Further conversation, as in Frank's case, often revealed that the loss of trees made other things that much harder to bear—more "foreign," as Lewis said.

When the fallen trees appeared more or less plainly personified—as in images of an "injured" or killed "friend"—that also reflected a loss of shelter, familiarity, companionship. For instance, Dan's job requires he be "out there with it [the devastation] day after day"—walking "day after day over the bodies of all those prostrate trees out there." It "has affected me in a way that few other things have." Dan later elaborated on the image of "bodies": "a wildlife technician who...does some contract work for us...came up with that image. He said it's like walkin' around over dead people...It does give you that feelin'."

NOTES

1. Gaston Bachelard, *Air and Dreams: An Essay on the Imagination of Movement,* trans. Edith R. and C. Frederick Farrell (Dallas, 1988), p. 217.

2. Phyllis Windle, "The Ecology of Grief," *BioScience,* 42, 5 (May 1992): pp. 363-366.

3. *Observer* staff, "Rare Trees Lost," *The London Observer* (Sunday, October 18, 1987), p. 1.

4. Mary Oliver, "The Lost Children," *American Primitive* (Boston, 1984), p. 15.

5. Mary Oliver, "Rain," in *The Best American Poetry 1992,* ed. Charles Simic (New York, 1992), pp. 149-153.

6. Carson McCullers, *The Ballad of the Sad Café and Other Stories* (New York, 1990 [1951]), 12. Following quotes from pp. 6, 12, 27, 70.

7. Carson McCullers, *The Heart Is A Lonely Hunter* (New York, 1967 [1940]), p. 244.

8. Toni Morrison, *Beloved* (New York, 1987). The following quotes are from pp. 79, 6, 89, 87, 19, 35, 17.

9. Zora Neale Hurston, *Their Eyes Were Watching God* (New York, 1990 [1937]), p. 18.

10. Annie Dillard, *The Living* (New York, 1992), p. 50.

11. See Hal Hartzell, Jr., *The Yew Tree: A Thousand Whispers: Biography of a Species* (Eugene, Oregon, 1992).

12. David Rains Wallace, *Bulow Hammock: Mind in a Forest* (San Francisco, 1989), pp. 13-14.

13. Tim O'Brien, "How to Tell a True War Story," *The Things They Carried* (Boston, 1989), p. 80.

14. Quoted in Loring M. Danforth, *The Death Rituals of Rural Greece* (Princeton, 1982), p. 98.

15. J. R. R. Tolkien, *The Return of the King, Part III of The Lord of the Rings,* (New York, 1965), p. 374.

16. In the combined edition of *The Charleston News and Courier/Evening Post* of Saturday, September 23, 1989.

CHILDREN OF HELL

GREG MOGENSON

My mother groan'd, my father wept;
Into the dangerous world I leapt...
—William Blake[1]

The Abyss of Personalism

In *The Marriage of Heaven and Hell*, William Blake recounts an episode of active imagination in which he was taken by an angel to the edge of an infinite abyss and there shown the dread fate that he had supposedly prepared for himself with his heresies.[2] Holding to the roots of trees, the poet peered into the depths and there saw the horrors of the Christian Hell. Terrible though the vision was with its immense spiders, devil animals, scaly serpent and fires of blood, its traumatic impact was not sufficient to constrain his imagination or damn his soul. On the contrary, the moment the angel departed, the vision of hell faded and Blake found himself transported to a pastoral scene on a river bank. There a harper sang a song which linked the horrors which Blake had just witnessed to the angel's orthodox (we would now say, fundamentalist) mindset which, because it "never alters...opinions [,] is like standing water, &

Greg Mogenson is a psychotherapist in London, Ontario. He is the author of *God Is A Trauma: Vicarious Religion and Soul-Making*, and *Greeting the Angels: An Imaginal View of the Mourning Process*.

breeds reptiles in the mind."[3] Leaving the harper, Blake set out to find the angel. Surprised to see him, the angel asked how it was that he escaped from hell. "All...we saw was owing to your metaphysics,"[4] Blake replied. With this remark, the tables were turned. Catching hold of the angel, Blake took him "westerly thro' the night" to "the void between Saturn & the fixed stars"[5] and there showed him a host of theologians who had been turned into monkeys, bound in chains, eating the flesh off themselves and one another while reading Aristotle's *Analytics*. This, Blake insisted, was the fate which the angel had prepared for himself through his orthodoxy.

The psychotherapist, no less than Blake, is confronted with visions of Hell. Daily he is taken to the abyss edge of another's pain. Peering into the abyss he sees the horrors of the deep: absent fathers, faceless mothers, jealous siblings, perverted uncles. In the century and a half since Blake gazed into Hell, Hell's imagery has changed. No longer are spiders, devil-animals, and serpents among the images which there underpin the soul's deepest torment. In their place we now envision domestic atrocities: tearfully told episodes of drunken violence, mother's face, like Medusa's, casting a petrifying stare, and the impossibility of making father proud.

Freud's emphasis on the importance of childhood experiences has become such a cultural fashion that most people today understand themselves in terms of their familial background. Indeed, patients in therapy for the first time often make reference to family experiences from the outset of treatment with a sophistication that rivals that of patients who completed an analysis in their parents' generation. Ironically, while we have valued science for its supposedly de-mythologizing effect, its application to developmental psychology and family dynamics has made the family seem even more hellish.

Consider, for example, the founding cases—Dora, Little Hans, and the Wolfman. Immortalized in the annals of psychoanalysis these early patients have become the Titans of our age. As Freud imagined into their repressed experiences, so we construct our own. Dora swept up in the arms of Herr K., the sensation of his erect penis through her skirt, the disgust she felt over her own arousal, her ambivalent rebuff, her wish and her fear, are now so *a priori* a part of the psyche of modern women that such events no longer have the power to constellate (if they ever did) the hysteria they once explained. Or, put another way, the hysteria is now a collective phenomenon, constellated less by actual instances of rape and seduction (though these continue to occur as frequently as ever) than by the explanatory concepts which rape and seduction have now become.[6] Today the event in the alley at the hands of a stranger or in the bedroom at the hands of a babysitter, father or uncle have become as redundant as they are ubiquitous. For though the perpetrators continue to offend, in another sense they have already been caught. The professional literature of social work and psychology have established procedures for dealing with assault and family violence. The acts have already been dealt with, the impact on the victim explored. Psychology is no longer in people, it is in psychology. The soul which was once raped into awareness by the atrocities of actual life has been blinded by the hyper-awareness of the disciplines which are supposedly committed to its care. For Dora lives on, larger than life, the author of an incest workbook, the leader of a rape support group, the priestess of the mystery, a Ph.D. Her experience has become *the* experience. And just as Catholic believers once devoted themselves to the *Imitatio Christi*, so the sufferers of the *a priori* afflictions of our age devote themselves to the imitation of Dora (sexual assault), Anna O (hysteria), and Ellen West (schizophrenia/anorexia).

Hillman makes much the same point with regard to Little Hans. By designating this phobic five-year-old "a little Oedipus" on account of the boy's desire to usurp his father's place with respect to his mother, Freud, in Hillman's view, unwittingly "ennobled the family with a mythical dimension."[7] This ennobling of family, however, was by no means an ennobling of myth. Misled by the oracle of causality, Freud reduced the mythical figure of Oedipus to Little Hans, thereby usurping, even as he claimed of Oedipus, the generative power which had fathered him. No wonder Freud was so threatened by Jung's research into the mythological background of the mind. No wonder he rejected Jung's view of incest. To accept it would be to recognize himself as the bringer of the very scourge he sought to cure. A Teiresias-figure, Jung confronted Freud with his failure to distinguish between Polybus and Merope—the mother and father of our actual life (and Oedipus' adoptive parents)—and Laius and Jocasta—our archetypal parents (and Oedipus' birth ones). Unable to blind himself, unable, that is, to accept this insight, Freud, unlike his mythical forebear, continued to see his own crime in projection. When we read the case histories of psychoanalysis, we must recognize who it was that brought the scourge upon Vienna by confusing that city with Thebes. Hoist on the petard of his own theories, Freud himself was patient zero—the first neurotic of the twentieth century. And from him we move into negative numbers—Dora -1, Little Hans -2, the Wolfman -3 and so on down to the present age in which we now understand ourselves, not individually, but statistically, as insignificant members in a large sample. For though Freud's brilliance resided in his ability to explore his own psyche and to work creatively with the illness he found there, those who have sickened of themselves in the wake of Freud have been less able to work creatively with their sickness precisely because of what he did with his.

From the very beginning, psychoanalysis replaced the self-analysis from which it sprang. Only Freud, it was believed, was capable of engaging in a dialectical process of self-discovery on his own. Like a seal upon prophecy, his scientific writings placed a dogma upon the inner experience of those who followed after him. The chair in which he had sat alone grappling with the subject-object distinction—himself both the subject and the object of analysis—gave way in short order to two chairs, or rather a chair and a couch. And so it was that the soul became divided against itself, a self-for-others in the very place that promised to restore to it its relationship with itself. Rebelling against this tyranny, the dissidents Stekel, Adler, Rank, and Jung, each in their own way and for their own reasons, broke with Freud. Their purpose in doing so was not to steal the ideas of their forebear or to corrupt them, but to free themselves to be sick in creative ways of their own. As Jung put it, during his own period of self-analysis, a period which only properly began during his breakdown years following his withdrawal from the psychoanalytic association, "I failed to consider that the soul cannot be the object of my judgement and knowledge; rather my judgement and knowledge are the objects of my soul."[8] With this change of opinion, Jung released himself from the standing water that had been breeding reptiles in his mind.

The Wolfman, Freud's favorite patient, is yet another exemplar of our age. Though we may be unconvinced, despite Freud's masterful exposition, that the neurosis of this bankrupt Russian aristocrat began in early childhood with the spectacle of his parents performing "coitus *a tergo*"[9] in their Victorian bloomers, there can be little doubt of the fixating effect of Freud's view that it had. In the years following his sittings with Freud, the Wolfman became a career patient, arrested less by the scenes of his childhood than by the theories which Freud and his later analysts had developed about the significance of those scenes. For no matter how old the Wolfman became and no matter which life-cycle stage he might have otherwise attained, he remained what psychoanalysis told him he was: a neurotic child. Indeed, even today, years after his death, his patienthood continues, carried on by subsequent generations of patients even as Freud's work has been carried on by subsequent generations of analysts.

As we close out this century there can be no doubt that Freud was an epochal individual. Indeed, without exaggeration it can be stated that the entire Western world has been affected by his teachings. *A priori*, we have all lain upon the couch in his consulting room at Berggasse 19. Inheritors of cultural history, we are now born analyzed. No longer is it necessary to laboriously reconstruct from the "chaos of...unconscious memory traces... the picture of a coitus between [our] parents."[10] Today, everyone knows that they have been screwed up by their parents. Never mind that this is not quite what Freud intended. It is how his ideas have been absorbed. Just watch any talkshow. There you will see the extent to which the Wolfman's neurosis carries on. Though the viewing audience has replaced the individual patient, the associations are the same: Parents are toxic, childhood is hell, life has been ruined, others are to blame.

As we gaze into the abyss to which Freud, Kohut and the other angels of this age have led us it is difficult to recognize the extent to which it, too, is a function of the metaphysics of our time. Moved by accounts of the neglect, cruelty, and abuse which the nominal adult of our day—the so-called "adult child"—has suffered, we tend to swallow wholesale the notion that the wretchedness of their present lives is the result of their difficult beginnings. After all, common sense, the reservoir of collective feeling, has always maintained the importance of the family in the rearing of its young. "Raise up a child in the way that he should go," states a biblical adage. "As a tree is bent, so it grows."

There is nothing biblical, however, in the psychoanalytic reiteration of this age-old wisdom. Indeed, like the theologians in Blake's vision, who had been turned into monkeys by the same Aristotelian assumptions that had led Darwin to assert that man had descended from the ape, Freud, a godless Jew, reduced religion to the very same antecedents of infantile sexual life to which he had earlier reduced neurosis. Polarizing against Jung, who recognized in the symbolism of religion the lineaments of the objective psyche, Freud re-doubled his efforts to explain the psyche exclusively in terms of the causal-reductive assumptions of science. But when causality usurps religion, as it does in Freud and most subsequent psychology, the antecedents it places in its stead—mom, dad, and the child we once were—become as gods.

The contemporary decline of the family is a function of the same "impoverishment of symbolism" which Jung identified as the malaise responsible for our "rediscovery of the gods as psychic factors, that is as archetypes of the unconscious."[11] Where once we considered ourselves to be the children of God as well as of our parents, and experienced ourselves as being cradled as much by the culture as by our families (family itself a symbol pointing beyond itself to something inexpressible from which it drew its strength)[12], now it is up to individual family members to shore each other up against their ruin. Holding a child in one hand and a book on how to raise it in the other, parents today attempt to raise their secular-humanist progeny, quite overwhelmed by the task before them, despite an unprecedented understanding of attachment, development and family dynamics. Ironically, it is precisely here, in the obsessional worry of the "am-I-a-good-enough-mother," not to mention the increasing dependence on experts, that the gods return in negative form.

It is not merely that instinct has been lost. Culture has also declined. To invoke a biblical analogy, having eaten the latest peach from the tree of knowledge, we have been stripped once again of our cultural apparel, and are unable to ascend the tree of life. Impoverished of symbolism, naked and ashamed, we experience even the oldest and most rudimentary elements of domestic life from the point of view of the fall.

Given that our latest trespass on the tree of knowledge has been in the sphere of psychology, it is little wonder that psychology—for all its contemporary scientific rigor—so sensitizes us to the guilt of what was once called original sin. Every family is a failed Eden. Every family member a sinner. Never mind that we no longer believe such mythology. It is precisely our un-belief, or as Jung put it, our "impoverishment of symbolism," that burdens us with what the culture once carried.

Our society's notion of evil is a case in point. No longer the malevolent force which religious imagination had acquainted us with, Evil has become identical with empathic failure in interpersonal relationships. Lacking a god through which to establish a relationship to that portion of life and fate that transcends our human limitations, it is now up to us to number the hairs on each other's heads and to hear the sparrow fall. No wonder hell has become equivalent to other people.

As our empathic capacity becomes more and more overloaded by the psychoanalytic account of the hurt, cruelty, and abuse which people suffer, we do well to recognize that the supernatural containers which once helped to contain this suffering, and even initiated the soul through it, have been cast into disrepute by the same science from which psychoanalysis springs.

But what are our etiological theories really saying? When we fault the parents and then forgive them at a later stage out of a recognition that they have been failed by their forebears, generation after generation, are we not suggesting, in a deeper sense, that we have lost our relationship with the ancestral dimension of the soul?

With just a few strokes of its saw, personalistic psychology has severed the great chain of generations. First stroke: parents must provide their children, during the short period of ontogenetic development, with everything that they are phylogenetically predisposed to expect. Second stroke: there are no phylogenetic predispositions, in either parents or children to facilitate this process.

Of course, there is no denying that parental figures are important or, to use a better word, necessary. The question is, are they sufficient? We do well to keep in mind the philosophical usage of these terms, "necessary" and "sufficient," when we think of the child in relation to its family. Being dependent, children do, of necessity, rely on their parents. The necessity of having attachment figures, however, in no way implies that these attachment figures will be sufficient. Something beyond the personal may also be needed. The deep cultural substratum of the psyche, which Jung called the collective unconscious, might also be seen as a necessary, if not sufficient, conditioning factor. Being a parent requires that we again and again stretch ourselves beyond the limits of our social conditioning and usual personalities—something of an entirely different order from the mere performance of yet another instrumental task on behalf of our child. To put it in the language of the New Testament, we must, as parents, be born again and again like Nicodemus if we are to respond in concert with our children who are also the children of God.

Unfortunately, today's parents have been dislocated from this mystery to a large extent. Converts of a new faith which no longer recognizes powers beyond their own, they believe that they, as parents, must become the God(s) which their tradition no longer believes in. But this "strength of usurpation," which modern psychology has displayed through its usurpation of theology, is not a human strength. Nor is the supposedly all important mother-child bond itself the Great Chain of Being—despite the fact that it is stretched to the breaking point by the expectation that it be so. No wonder that "things fall apart." No wonder that "the centre cannot hold." Dislocated by the anti-metaphysics of our time from the ontological support which the culture once provided, burdened with having to be both the necessary and sufficient conditions of children (and by implication of the whole human enterprise), we resign from the responsibilities of family life. After all, we are only human.

The Dynamics of Grace

Were this power [of the archetype] really in our hands and subject to our will, we would be so crushed with responsibility that no one in his right senses would dare to have children.
—C.G. Jung[13]

In two deceptively simple poems, "The Little Boy Lost" and "The Little Boy Found," William Blake succinctly describes the interrelationship between the personal and suprapersonal aspects of the psyche. On the one hand, the simplicity of these poems serves to communicate something of the role grace plays in ordinary life, and, on the other, it serves to parody the priestly account of grace. In Blake's view, the priestly account, far from saving the soul or freeing it to a more abundant life, inscribes it with a tyranny.

Reading the first of these poems, the contemporary reader is immediately transported to the abyss edge of the symbol-impoverished, personalistic psychology which we described in the previous section.

The Little Boy Lost

"Father! father! where are you going?
"O do not walk so fast.
"Speak, father, speak to your little boy,
"Or else I shall be lost."

The night was dark, no father was there;
The child was wet with dew;
The mire was deep, & the child did weep,
And away the vapour flew.[14]

The little boy's plaintive cry resonates at once with our present day concern with absent fathers and neglected sons. We think of single parent households and weekend dads, the psychopathic boyfriends of the needy welfare mother and the fatherless gangs of the ghetto—to say nothing of the ubiquitously absent peripheral father ("workaholic," "alcoholic," "cold, remote and ineffectual") of our psychotherapeutic case histories.

The forlorn image of abandonment with which the poem ends resonates as well with our modern notion of the child as the victim of empathic failure, parental neglect, cruelty and abuse. We think of "hurried" children driven to achieve by perfectionistic parents, "latch-key" children bonded to the television set, and the poor little rich kids whom Kohut analyzed, even as Blake thought of the little chimney sweeps, vagabonds and child-laborers of his own day.

Of course, there can be no doubt that Blake intended to evoke in his readers the same feelings of inconsolate dejection to which the little boy is subjected in the poem. The degree to which this evocation of feeling succeeds with the poem's contemporary readership, however, must certainly be well in excess of the poet's nineteenth century expectations. For the reader of today is already well acquainted with this poor little waif from other sources. Freud, Kohut, and Alice Miller, to name but several analytic authors, have all acquainted us with him, each in different aspects. Popular culture has also focussed attention on this figure. Indeed, he appears, as we have already mentioned, almost daily on television talkshows, as if he were the very spirit of the age.

Compared to the lost child which we know from these sources, Blake's portrayal seems understated and naive. For, in addition to being deserted, we now know or imagine that the little boy has been beaten, incested, enmeshed, parentified, thwarted, unsatisfactorily educated, misunderstood, kidnapped, molested, raped and killed.

Looking back to Blake's portrayal, however, we can readily gage the extent to which the empathic imagination of our day has become identified with and overdetermined by this one motif. Today there is a hurt in every child and a child in every hurt. Put another way, the two ideas, "hurt" and "child," have been fused together into a single complex, a complex, moreover, which functions as an *a priori* perceptual category, an angel of orthodoxy—like the one that took Blake to the edge of the abyss—an archetypal image. Although we may assume that the image of the lost boy or abandoned child is an imaginal accretion built up from numerous experiences of actually being hurt and abused (phylogenetically or ontogenetically), the opposite may also be true. *Inasmuch as the abandoned child has become an autonomous cultural complex, our sense of having been neglected, hurt, and abused may be merely the overdetermined effect of its particular manner of turning events into experiences.* Is the boy in the poem, the child-in-the-patient, the victim on the talkshow *caused* by abusive events, or are the events in question merely *viewed* as having been abusive because we experience them from the perspective of this inner figure? Do we suffer from fixation (Freud) or regression (Jung), or some combination of the two?

Turning now to the companion poem, "The Little Boy Found," let us first note that the very supplement of reading which enlarges beyond measure the modern reader's sensitivity to the plight of the deserted boy, dampens to the point of extinction that same reader's sensitivity to the numinous experience to which the little boy is later subject.

> The Little Boy Found
>
> The little boy lost in the lonely fen,
> Led by the wand'ring light,
> Began to cry; but God, ever nigh,
> Appear'd like his father in white.
>
> He kissed the child & by the hand led
> And to his mother brought,
> Who in sorrow pale, thro' the lonely dale,
> Her little boy weeping sought.[15]

It is not the first lines that give us trouble. Indeed, they simply take up where the first poem left off. While wandering "lost in a lonely fen," the little boy despairs and begins crying. Again, we have no trouble empathizing with his forlorn state. It is the subsequent lines that the contemporary reader has difficulty grasping. As the poem continues, we learn that despite there being no one present to hear the little boy, and despite his seeming to be utterly abandoned, "God, ever nigh,/Appear[s] like his father in white," kisses him and then leads him by the hand back to the keep of his pale, sorrowful mother.

To the contemporary reader, the second poem seems to trivialize the very horrors which the first poem had depicted. Indeed, compared to all that is now known about the mistreatment of children, the notion that "God, ever nigh" watches over the lost boy reads like a pious platitude. Not only does the poem's matter of fact affirmation of the belief that God is in his heaven and all is right with the world gloss over the very experiences which make such an assertion a matter of doubt. As an answer to the theological problem of how human suffering is to be squared with a loving God, it merely begs the question. To those for whom God's grace is no longer a self-evident truth and for whom belief in God is waning or absent, such a matter of fact affirmation of God as the remedy for human affliction is tantamount to saying that such affliction does not exist. Placebo effects notwithstanding, the suggestion that a vacuous hypostasis or nominal phantom can miraculously save the lost little boy from the misfortune which has befallen him implies to the modern reader that the little boy's misfortune was inconsequential to begin with. The very credulity that facilitates belief in the "ever-nigh" God depicted in the poem impedes our recognition of the atrocities to which children are subjected. More darkly, what would appear to be credulity may in fact be a cover for hypocrisy of the most wicked sort. Indeed, when one considers the fact that priests are now numbered among the most frequent abusers of young boys, the idea of God's providence is particularly hard to swallow.

Is it really God who is ever-nigh, or is it denial? The contemporary reader, desensitized to the reality of God by the same supplement of reading that has sensitized him to the misuse of children, suspects the latter to be the case. The theophanic resolution of the little boy's plight is suggestive of a defensive deployment of the imagination. Incapable of the anxiety and depressive despair which were evoked earlier, the poem, given over to mechanisms familiar to us from Freudian dream theory, resorts to wish-fulfillment. Negative affect is defensively idealized. The deflated, worthless self merges with the grandiose other. The forlorn ego identifies with the persecutory anxiety to which it had previous felt exposed. The traumatic stressor, whatever it may have been, is now propitiated as if it were God.[16] The soul's pathology is transcendentally denied.[17]

Less darkly, but still within the confines of a personalistic psychology, the appearance of God may reflect that the boy in the poem, like the child-in-the-patient, is experiencing the process which Kohut called "transmuting internalization."[18] From this point of view, the little boy's abandonment may be more apparent than real, and his rescue, by the same token, more human than divine. Indeed, the very fact that the little boy is rescued, would, for Kohut, suggest that what he subjectively experienced as abandonment was merely a momentary lapse (or "optimal frustration") in the empathic attunement of his "good enough" parent. Such momentary lapses, in Kohut's view, far from being ruinous, compel the child or patient to imitatively provide for him or herself the soothing and esteem which the parent, therapist or other outer figure had previously provided. Though the little boy's relationship with his father has been discontinuous, or rather, precisely because of this, he has been able to establish a more cohesive self-structure. The appearance at the end of the poem of the heavenly father reflects that the little boy is able to take over something of the function of his earthly father. He is now able to father himself.

Without contesting the validity of any of these readings, let us now turn our attention to the suprapersonal experience which the poem presents. Blake, as we mentioned at the outset of this section, wrote these poems to parody the priestly account of redemption. Like the contemporary reader, he, too, found the doctrine of grace trite, not, however, because there was no God, but because God resided in the very abyss from which the priestly view of grace (i.e., empathic attunement of the good-enough Church) would save us. In Blake's view, it is in precisely those states of despair and affliction where we feel most dislocated from God that we are most likely to encounter Him. God "ever-nigh" means, for Blake, that God is never more numinously present than in what we experience to be his absence. In this regard, the plaintive cry of the little boy lost resonates with the cry of the crucified Jesus, "My God, my God, why hast thou forsaken me" (Matt. 27:46). Abandonment, such as the lost boy suffers in the poems and our patients' suffer in their families, plays a crucial role in religious experience. For until we are abandoned, we live in the false security of our assumptive identities, questioning neither our views of self and other or our views of personal and supra-personal, theology's ego usurping religion's soul.[19]

Case Examples

The following case examples, drawn from my former practice as a family therapist, play out the same redemption motif as does Blake's poem.

A single mother consulted me about her six-year-old daughter's refusal to attend school. Each day she would walk her daughter to the school yard, but would be unable to leave her there. For, like the little lost boy of Blake's poem, her daughter would cling to her the moment she turned to go and cry out, "Mother! where are you going? Mother, don't leave me." Looking at her wailing child, the young mother would lose her resolve, take the girl by the hand, and lead her home with vague hopes of succeeding the next day.

Of course, the problem was the mother's, not the little girl's. She, too, felt upset at the prospect of separating from her daughter. It had been just the two of them from the beginning. They had been as one. The thought of going home for those few hours without her daughter made her feel empty and afraid. Her daughter's plaintive cry was merely the echo of her own. She, too, was a little girl, the little girl of her little girl. She, too, felt abandoned.

There was a boyfriend. The relationship with him seemed to have the same dynamics as her relationship with her daughter, except that he felt engulfed and was now moving away from her. Like the little boy lost, she beseeched him not to leave her, but, like the father in the poem, he seemed indifferent to her sorrow. Unable to hold onto him she held onto her daughter all the tighter. But this was not enough to fill the emptiness she felt inside.

As this therapy hour, the first of four, continued, the story became darker. She was beside herself about her boyfriend, ruminating about him much of the time. She had thoughts of taking her life. None of this was lost on the daughter. Indeed, she had clearly taken on the role of driving off her mother's depression. Mostly this consisted of trying to cheer her mother up. When this did not work the girl attempted to pull her mother out of her symptoms by manifesting symptoms of her own.

Just as Blake's vision of the horrors awaiting him in hell was a function of the metaphysical assumptions of the angel of orthodoxy, my understanding of the horrors suffered by this family were, until this point, a function of the theories of Mahler, Masterson, and Minuchin—the angels of my therapeutic orthodoxy. However, when the young mother began to tell me about her recent experience of being unable to stay in her pew at church, I, like Blake, was taken away from these perspectives by quite another kind of harper. I found myself thinking about the spiritual malaise Kierkegaard described as the "sickness unto death."

The Sunday before our session, while sitting in church, the young mother was overwhelmed by the incongruity between the gaiety of the service and the state of her own soul. She felt wretched and alone. If God was as benevolent as the hymns affirmed, why did he not help her? she asked herself. Why did he allow her to suffer? Leaving the sanctuary in the middle of the service, even as Blake left the Church of his own day, the young woman went to her car and waited for her daughter to finish Sunday school. Her thoughts oscillated between anger at God for neglecting her and dread that He did not exist. Recounting this incident to me she seemed to re-enter the same abyss of despair.

It was at this point in her story that I found myself thinking of Kierkegaard. In Kierkegaard's view, "The decisive thing is that for God all things are possible."[20] God, as most believers vacuously affirm, is, indeed, "ever-nigh." However, our recognition of this, our faith, as it were, is limited by the expectancy and hope we place in ourselves and others. As Kierkegaard put it:

> [T]he decisive affirmation comes only when a man is brought to the utmost extremity, so that humanly speaking no possibility exists. Then the question is whether he will believe that for God all things are possible—that is to say, whether he will believe. But this is completely the formula for losing one's mind or understanding; to believe is precisely to lose one's understanding in order to win God.[21]

Sitting in her car outside the church, the young mother was on the brink of despair. I say, "on the brink," because she still had a shred of hope. She would be meeting me the next day. After she had finished repudiating her Maker, she looked up at me, as if expecting a tender, reassuring word. Realizing that she could very easily mistake me for the redeemer, I withstood the impulse to lean forward in my chair. "Salvation," I said to myself, recalling the words of Kierkegaard, "is humanly speaking the most impossible thing of all; but for God all things are possible!"[22] In order to help this woman, I realized, I must betray her expectation that help lay in my direction.

"That is a grim story," I said to her at length. "Your life has become impossible. Your lover has left you. You feel empty and alone. Your Church trivializes your despair. No one understands. Many have tried to help you, but that has only kept you small. The road to hell is paved with good intentions. You hope that I can help, and though I like you and will walk with you for awhile, I don't have the answer. For you have come to the end of yourself. People can't help. Suicide can't help. And now you blame God, though it would seem you have believed in everything except God. You have believed in your boyfriend, your Church, your daughter, death. Now that you have despaired of all these things, now that you have recognized that salvation is humanly impossible, perhaps you will now begin to sense the spirit of God."

As I spoke these lines, particularly the last lines about God, I felt an uncanny sensation surge through me. Although all I had said was consistent with the techniques of modern suggestive therapy (utilization of the symptom, speaking the client's language, interdicting previous solution behavior, re-framing, etc.), and although I had long prided myself in my skill in this area, the uncanny sensation I experienced each time I found myself speaking of God to this woman suggested to me that what was taking place was not magic, but miracle, not technique but grace.

The word "impossible" seemed very apt to the young mother. Unhappy as she was she seemed to rejoice in its accuracy. There was nothing she could do but surrender to the realization of the impossibility of her situation. She talked about the Church, about how there was nothing for her there. I replied that God was in her car, in the despair she had felt while in her car, and again felt that uncanny feeling. On and on we talked. She confessed how empty she felt and how immature. She confessed that she had never been able to bear being alone. Each night she went to sleep at the same time as her daughter, eight o'clock, unable to bear being awake by herself. "God," I suggested, "was one minute past eight o'clock." He would also be there, we concluded, when she refrained from calling her boyfriend.

The young mother was immediately able to make use of these ideas. The abyss of despair which she had sought to avoid by merging with others she now recognized to be the place of the Lord. Though she continued to experience loneliness, she could now inhabit it, for God was with her. In each of the three subsequent sessions, she reported an increased capacity to "spend more time with God." She no longer felt compelled to call her boyfriend, her interest in him lessening as she herself became more robust. She was able to smile at her daughter at the school yard gate, thereby filling the girl with enough good feelings to separate and attend class. She began to pursue interests of her own, rather than clinging to other people. As with the little boy in Blake's poem, it was by losing her way that she found or was found by God.

Another mother-daughter case from my practice also illustrates something of what I have called in this paper the dynamics of grace. After the birth of her first and, to date, only child, this young wife and mother suffered a severe, post-partum depression. Overwhelmed by the needs of her infant daughter, or, rather, by her own anxious fantasies about her daughter's needs, she made a number of near-lethal suicide attempts. The rationale behind these gestures was one of altruistic sacrifice. If she were able end to her life while her daughter was still an infant her husband would be able to remarry, thereby providing their daughter with a new and more suitable mother-figure with whom to become attached. The renewal of her motherhood, however, was not to be achieved in this manner.

The family was referred to me shortly after the mother's release from the psychiatric hospital. She had been an in-patient there for approximately eight months. It had clearly been a shattering experience. The doctors and nurses, in her view, had failed her, just as she had failed, and could only continue to fail, her daughter. She had no faith that she was or could be good enough for her daughter, a sentiment clearly rooted in the deficiencies of her own childhood. Every act she preformed with respect to her daughter, she found wanting and felt guilty about. If she helped her daughter with a task, she believed she was thwarting her, and if she tried to support the girl's autonomy, she felt that she was neglecting or abandoning her. Although she had read numerous parenting books and had attended many parenting classes, everything seemed to contradict everything else. On the one hand, she experienced her daughter as an abusive tyrant, and, on the other, as the innocent victim of her bad mothering. She could not bear to be with her daughter or to be apart from her. There was literally no place she could be without feeling bad. The mother imago was decidedly negative.

Therapy was intensive and long term, involving, successively, family sessions to help the father to recognize and assume his parenting role, sessions with the mother and daughter to ameliorate the anxiety which underpinned their ambivalent attachment style, twice a week analytically-oriented psychotherapy with the mother to address her personality disorder, and finally marital therapy. Of this work, I wish to report the events of a single session with the mother.

In the third year of our work together the mother told me what she thought to be a damning story about herself. The day before she had been out in the park with her daughter, who was now three years old. While the girl played contentedly in the sand, she anxiously poured over one of her parenting books. She was just beginning to appreciate another crucial feature of child-rearing and to measure herself negatively against it, when all of a sudden her daughter uttered a terrified shriek. Two boys of about six or seven years of age, who had been playing on the climbers near by, were now throwing handful after handful of gravel directly into her daughter's face. Dropping her book, the mother catapulted to her daughter's aid. Placing herself protectively between the boys and her daughter, she grabbed hold of the nearest of the two rascals and told him in no uncertain terms that he had no business throwing stones at her daughter.

"You see!" she said to me with an anguished expression on her face, "I'm no good. I'm violent, like my father! I try not to get angry. I was so scared of his anger. But I'm just like him! It is just as the books say, we parent as we were parented, the abused child becomes a child abuser!"

As I listened to my patient condemn herself, I found myself thinking once again about Blake and the hell that he had supposedly prepared for himself with his heresies. This woman's hell, it seemed to me, was every bit as much a function of the metapsychological assumptions of our time as Blake's vision was a function of the metaphysical assumptions of his day. While there can be no doubt that the abuse she suffered as a child, and which she was now introducing into the therapy through discussion of this incident, had been harmful to her, she was, or so I felt, even more harmed by the significance which contemporary psychological theories ascribe to such factors. Indeed, when we consider that she *had* acted to protect her child, but was unable to recognize that fact due to the psychological truism which held that she was damned to raise her child as poorly as she had been raised by her parents, we must ask ourselves if the neurosis was in her or in psychology.

While in the first case, it had been Kierkegaard who had freed me from the hell to which personalistic psychological theories might otherwise have assigned the therapy, in this case it was Jung. Indeed, as the young mother continued to pathologize herself, I found myself recalling his ideas about the purposive meaning or redemptive potential of neurotic infantilism.

In Jung's view, infantile material, such as my patient was now presenting, is the regressive product of the failure to adapt to one's present reality. The libido reverts to themes from the past, not so much because it was been fixated there as Freud maintained, but because consciousness does not have the means at its disposal to resolve the current dilemma which would allow it to move forward. Developmental deficits notwithstanding, regression, for Jung, is not in itself a pathological occurrence. Indeed, if followed back to the deeper layers of the psyche which are "beyond the sphere of personal psychology," it may "activat[e] collective images (archetypes) which have a compensatory and curative meaning..."[23] This, I believe, is what had happened to my patient on the playground. Despite her neurotic uncertainty, or, rather, precisely because of it, she was able to access, through regression, the instinctual pattern of behavior which was appropriate to her situation. Again, by regression, Jung did not mean merely a return to the vicissitudes of early childhood—although the repudiation of childhood is perhaps the most common rebirth motif met with in psychotherapeutic practice. The redemptive potential of regression resides in those reaches of the unconscious which are anterior to the family romance.

Complaints about the family, however justified, are also instances of what Jung called "autochthonous revival."[24] The capacity to regress to more infantile states of being and to complain about one's early life is underpinned by a primordial awareness that things could have been or should have been otherwise, a nostalgia for the archetype. Unlike the mythical hero of by-gone days, the anti-hero of today differentiates from the parental imagos, not by slaying them as in the dragon fight, but through forensically substantiated allegations of having been slayed by them—abused, neglected, abandoned. But what would seem at first glance to be an infantile rejection of one's actual life, may reveal itself, upon closer scrutiny, to be the acceptance into life of the energies and instincts which had hitherto been missing from it. The remedy is already present in the symptom itself. The neurosis, as Jung said, is an attempt at self cure.[25]

The deficits of my patient's childhood, deficits which she spoke of in terms of the poor modelling which her parents had provided, correspond to those "gaps in childhood memory," which, in Jung's view, "are merely the symptoms of a much greater loss—the loss of the primitive psyche."[26] While personalistic psychologies, suffering the same neurosis as the patient, seek for the solution of the patient's problem in the dim memories of childhood, the solution actually lies in the childhood of the species, or as Jung put it, in the "primitive psyche." While it is true that childhood experiences influence later development, the psyche cannot be reduced to these experiences without remainder. Indeed, the remainder is so huge—just divide three million by five—that we must reckon the influence of the primitive psyche to be at least as important if not decidedly more important than family experiences.

My job with this young mother was to help her to understand, with Jung, that "an infantile memory gap...represents a positive loss,"[27] and that the deficits of her childhood, far from destroying her capacity to mother, were her link to the compensatory potential of the collective unconscious, the objective psyche, the original, primitive mind. Though her childhood had been ruined by abuse, and though this complicated her adult life in many ways, the suprapersonal dimension of the psyche was not harmed. When the situation necessitated action, a wholesome, instinctual reaction spontaneously occurred. The patient *had* acted to protect her daughter. There *was* something good in her from which her daughter had benefited and could continue to benefit. What's more, this good had come out of the apparent badness of her personal incapacity.[28]

"Unmediated reactions of mothering," writes Hillman, "are complicated by mediated ideas or fantasies, about good and bad mothering."[29] Though my patient had spontaneously risen to the mothering challenge with which she had been presented, collective ideas about good or bad mothering interfered with her recognition of this fact. As I listened, I felt tempted to brush aside her self-critical statements, and simply celebrate her spontaneous action. Such an intervention, however, would have remained on the level of suggestion. Much as I valued her unmediated reaction, and hoped that she might value it too, spiriting away her sense of bad with my sense of good would only keep her locked in the metaphysics of bad and good. As Hillman has put it, "bad mothering takes its definition from the oppositional effect of tandem logic."[30]

As I continued to listen to my patient, I asked myself what the psyche's purpose might be in re-doubling this mother's sense of badness. Perhaps, I reflected, the badness was a necessary part of the mothering and needed to be given credit as well.

"Human beings worry that they are bad mothers," I said to her at last. "They worry so much that they actually cut themselves off from their mothering capabilities. But mother bears do not worry. They just follow their instincts, as you did on the playground. It is a good thing bears can't read. Imagine a mother bear thumbing through the index of a parenting book trying to find out what some expert has to say about the proper procedure to follow when two boys are tormenting her cub. Well, I'll bet those boys will know better next time not to get between a mother bear and her cub! I'm glad that you are bad enough at doing the 'proper' thing, the politically correct thing, that mother nature has a chance to enter in. She does seem to be there for you when the boys and the parenting books come between you and your child."

Though therapy was to continue for several years, this session was a turning point. The notion that she herself was being mothered by the archetype immediately seemed to diminish the sense of inadequacy she felt before her daughter. Now that she recognized the vulnerable child in herself, she ceased to project that figure so exclusively upon her daughter. Just as the lost boy of Blake's poem was found by God, this mother was found by the positive aspect of the mother archetype, despite the fact, or rather, precisely because of the fact that previously she had negatively identified with it. In subsequent sessions, she described how important the large trees near where she had taken to walking had become to her. They were huge oak trees. Older than she was, they would probably outlive her. They had a quality of timelessness or eternity. And most important, they were not anxious. Her concerns could be carried in their branches. As they soothed her with their rocking motion so she could soothe her daughter.

Beyond the Oedipus-complex

Freud was of the opinion that all "divine" figures have their
roots in the father-imago. It can hardly be denied that they do
derive from this imago, but what we say about the father-
imago is another matter. For the parental imago is possessed of
quite extraordinary power; it influences the psychic life of the
child so enormously that we must ask ourselves whether we
may attribute such magical power to an ordinary human being
at all. Obviously he possesses it, but we are bound to ask
whether it is really his property. Man "possesses" many things
which he has never acquired but has inherited from his ancestors. He is not born a *tabula rasa*, he is merely born unconscious.

—C.G. Jung[31]

   The Blake poems and the family therapy cases which we have
just examined each suggest that the principle relationships of our
lives, our relationships with immediate family members, are underpinned or understudied by another relationship, our relationship with that imago of the psyche which the pious call God. In
this regard, the poem and case examples are reminiscent of the
lyrics of the well-known negro spiritual, "He's got the whole
world in His hands." Though sung by the Christian faithful with
great evangelical zeal, this spiritual may serve to refocus our efforts to psychologically discriminate the interrelationship of the
personal and suprapersonal dimensions of the psyche.
   Hymns and spirituals of affirmation often come from calamities which have been embraced as providence and thereby survived. Not the least of these are the calamities of family life we
have just described. They, too, are worthy of a stanza in the
spiritual, for they, too, resolved themselves through surrender to
a higher power. True, the little boy who had lost track of his
father and the mothers who presented difficulties with their
daughters did not relate their stories with the robustness of an

Ella Fitzgerald singing this spiritual. However, the despair to which they were each subject was latent with similar lyrics:

> He's got you and me, mother, in His Hands.
> He's got you and me, father, in His Hands.
> He's got you and me, daughter, in His hands.
> He's got the whole world in His hands.

Of course, the God to whom this spiritual refers, the God who found the lost little boy and who helped each of the mothers more than any therapy could, was not the god whom Freud confessed his faith in in *The Future of an Illusion*. Indeed, from the point of view of Freud's god, Logos (Reason),[32] the God who holds the family members in His hands is nothing more than a grandiose Oedipal bogey. Unable to accept the limits which necessity and nature impose, and unable to tolerate the hostile forces of the environment, religious man, according to Freud, invents his God with reference to a prototype from infantile life: the personal father. Just as we had feared and longed for our father as children, and just as we identified with him in order not to have him as a foe, so in adulthood we resort to the same ingratiating tactics when faced with other forces before which we are similarly helpless. As Freud put it:

> ...when man personifies the forces of nature he is again following an infantile model. He has learnt from the persons in his earliest environment that the way to influence them is to establish a relation with them; and so, later on, with the same end in view, he treats everything else that he comes across in the same way as he treated those persons.[33]

In contrast to our spiritual's faithful affirmation that God, ever nigh, holds us in His hands, Freud argues that it is we who attempt to hold God, or rather, those overpowering forces which we personify as God, in our hands by relating to them in such a personal, familial manner.

Without directly disputing Freud's claim that it is not God who is ever-nigh, but the Oedipus-complex, let us continue our attempt to discriminate God, or, rather, the God-complex, from the family constellation to which psychoanalysis has reduced it.

As the quotation at the beginning of this section indicates, Jung also maintained that god-images and divine figures derive from the father-imago. In contrast to Freud, however, he did not see the father-imago as identical with, reducible to, or derived from the personal father. On the contrary, from Jung's perspective, our experience of having a father or of being a father is overdetermined by precisely that class of god-images which Freud attempted to reductively explain away through reference to the Oedipus-complex.

The term father-imago, in Jung's usage, designates a form belonging to all humanity. As such it is not something we acquire through the events of our personal history, but, rather, it is an inherited predisposition to experience those events in a particular way. Simply by virtue of being a father, a man is imbued with a whole host of potential attributes and an aura of numinosity. It does not matter whether he is a particularly worthy specimen. Even if he is the so-called weak, ineffectual father of our modern case histories, he is still suffused with the power of the imago, albeit it in negative form. Again, as we have already heard from Jung, though the personal father "obviously possesses [this magical power]...we are bound to ask whether it is really his property."

Deconstruction literary theory maintains that the words of a text are not a function of the objects which they appear to signify, but rather, of other signifiers, other words. A similar claim can be made for the words with which we address one another in the course of our day to day family life. Although the relationship between the word "father!", as in the cry to be fathered, is not totally discontinuous with the man we call our father, it is so overdetermined with archetypal resonances that the social connection it seeks to establish ruptures toward the recognition that in a larger sense it is a symbol.[34] Like the little boy lost, a son's or daughter's cry to be parented is not wholly answerable by the actual mother and father. Indeed, the actual parents are but the echo chambers in which the transpersonal depths of this cry resound.[35] It is in this sense that family is the wilderness in which we cry out for God.

Of course, it frequently happens that the actual parents so identify with the power of the archetype that they "exert a dominating influence on the child by way of suggestion."[36] When this happens it is more difficult for the subject to distinguish the suprapersonal dimension of the parental imagos from the actual parents, with the consequence that he or she remains galvanized by the influence of the family well into adult life. If, however, the subject is able to project the imago onto someone who values the projection but does not identify with it, a mentor or therapist perhaps, it may be possible for the projection to be seen through and a relationship to what Jung called a "transpersonal control-point"[37] forged.

Jung reports a case in which he was able to facilitate this experience in a young woman whose adult life was circumscribed by her relationship with her father. Though she initially endowed Jung with the attributes of a father-lover, subsequent dreams and fantasies granted him the qualities of a deity. The turning point of the therapy was reflected in a dream in which the patient dreamt that her father was a giant standing in the midst of a windswept wheat-field. Like the God of the spiritual who holds us in his hands, this giant father, who was also the ripening wheat and the wind, rocked her to and fro in his arms. From this and other experiences Jung concluded that the "unconscious was trying to *create* a god out of the person of the doctor, as it were to free a vision of God from the veils of the personal."[38]

The God which the unconscious creates through the transference is *not* Oedipal. Its authority is not the authority of the actual parents (though they are deputized to carry it for a time) and its constellation cannot be put down to the lingering effect of an infantile attitude. On the contrary, it is an imago in its own right and as such confronts our Oedipal identity and infantile attitude with the same crisis of vision that Jesus confronted Nicodemus with in the gospels:

> That which is born of the flesh is flesh, and that which is born of the Spirit is spirit. Do not marvel that I said to you, "You must be born again." The wind blows where it wishes and you hear the sound of it, but do not know where it comes from and where it is going; so is everyone who is born of the Spirit (John 3: 6-8).

Born of the spirit, children of God, we are no longer subject to the Oedipal confusion between the parental imagos and the actual parents. Having discriminated the suprapersonal dimension of the psyche from its first carriers in our lives, we are liberated from the *participation mystique* or unconscious identity which causes the themes of infanticide, parricide and incest to be played out in the family. Like Christ, who promised regeneration to "everyone who has left houses or brothers or sisters or father or mother or children or farms for My name's sake" (Matt. 19: 29), we know what it means to be born of a virgin and to have a heavenly father. With the realization that we "cannot in all fairness load that enormous burden of meaning, responsibility, duty, heaven and hell, onto the shoulders of one frail and fallible human being—so deserving of love, indulgence, understanding and forgiveness—[as she] who was our mother,"[39] our relationship to our mother, or for that matter, to our father and other significant persons, becomes transparent to a source of identity that is wholly other and yet, at the same time, closer to us than we are to ourselves.

Conclusion

In the episode of active imagination recounted at the beginning of this paper, Blake released himself from a hellish vision of his fate through a critique of the metaphysical assumptions which underpinned that vision. This paper, likewise, has attempted to release psychology from the personalism to which it has damned itself. Though the harrowing of the family is the contemporary counterpart to the harrowing of hell, the imagos which we project upon family members in the course of our struggle with them, being forms belonging to all humanity, necessitate a shift in our metapsychological assumptions.

Contrary to Freud, who reduced God to the Oedipus-complex, we, following Jung, have suggested that family psychology is overdetermined by the suprapersonal dimension of the psyche. Though we cannot know anything about God in a metaphysical sense, god-images analogous to the representations of God in religious traditions play a decisive role in our psychic life. These images, as analytical psychologists have repeatedly shown, present the psyche in its archetypal aspect. Neither we nor our parents can lay claim to having created them. On the contrary, as the a priori structures which underpin awareness, they create us.

Identity is not merely a function of the inter-relationship of nature and nurture. It has a "creationist" aspect as well. There is a life behind consciousness, a life which both precedes and provides for the emergence of the subject. Just as God engaged the biblical patriarchs in a dialectical relationship and through that relationship gradually initiated His people into their true identity, the empirical god-image, though itself perhaps no more than a psychic factor, provides a "counterposition to the subjective ego because it is a piece of the objective psyche."[40]

In a frequently quoted passage, Jung defines "religions as psychotherapeutic systems in the truest sense of the word, and on the grandest scale [because] they express the whole range of the psychic problem in mighty images."[41] Following Jung, it has been the contention of this paper that the reduction of these mighty images to the psychodynamics of the family not only wrongs religion, but the family as well. Parents dissipating into their symptomatic children, adults unable to see past the figures of Mom and Dad, the nullification of the individual and our modern cult of blame: might we not approach these problems differently if we remembered the Apocryphal adage: "It is a terrible thing to fall into the hands of the living God"?

Though we lament the breakdown of our family relationships and attribute to this breakdown the bulk of our psychic ills, it is in fact the breakdown of what Jung called the "great relationship,"[42] the breakdown, that is to say, of our relationship to the *imago dei*, which is responsible for that contemporary malaise we call neurosis. Cure of this malaise depends upon the recognition that despite the fact that the family can be a disturbed and disturbing social institution, it is also, even in its apparent ruin, "transparent to transcendence" (Joseph Campbell). This fact, entirely ignored by personalistic psychologies, is of the utmost importance, for as Jung said:

> The individual will never find the real justification of his existence, and his own spiritual and moral autonomy, anywhere except in an extramundane principle capable of relativizing the overpowering influence of external factors. The individual not anchored in God can offer no resistance on his own resources to the physical and moral blandishments of the world. For this he needs the evidence of inner, transcendental experience which alone can protect him from the otherwise inevitable submersion in the mass.[43]

NOTES

1. William Blake, *Selected Poetry and Prose of Blake*, ed. Northrop Frye (New York: Random House, 1953), p. 56.

2. *Ibid.*, pp. 130-132.

3. *Ibid.*, p. 131.

4. *Ibid.*

5. *Ibid.*, p. 132.

6. James Hillman, "Oedipus Revisited," in K. Kerenyi and James Hillman, *Oedipus Variations* (Dallas: Spring Publications, 1991), p. 140.

7. *Ibid.*, p. 98.

8. Paul. J. Stern, *C.G. Jung: The Haunted Prophet* (New York: Dell Publishing, 1976), p. 121.

9. Sigmund Freud, "From the History of an Infantile Neurosis," *Collected Papers* Vol III, tr. Alix and James Strachey (London: The Hogarth Press and The Institute of Psychoanalysis, 1950), p. 508.

10. *Ibid.*, p. 507.

11. C. G. Jung, *CW* 9, i, §50.

12. Hillman attempts to return us to a sense of the symbolic function of family by a revaluing of its so-called pathologies in his essay, "Extending the Family: From Entrapment to Embrace," *The Texas Humanist* 7/4 (1985): pp. 6-11.

13 C.G. Jung, *CW* 4, §729.

14. William Blake, *op. cit.*, p. 27.

15. *Ibid.*

16. Greg Mogenson, *God Is a Trauma: Vicarious Religion and Soul-Making* (Dallas: Spring Publications, 1989).

17. James Hillman, *Re-Visioning Psychology* (New York: Harper & Row, 1975), pp. 64-67.

18. Heinz Kohut, *How Does Analysis Cure?* (Chicago: University of Chicago Press, 1984), pp. 70-71.

19. David L. Miller, "Theology's Ego/Religion's Soul," in *Spring 1980*, pp. 78-88.

20. S. Kierkegaard, *Fear And Trembling and The Sickness Unto Death*, tr. Walter Lowrie (Princeton: Princeton University Press, 1968), p. 171.

21. *Ibid.*

22. *Ibid.*

23. C. G. Jung, *CW* 5, §655.

24. C. G. Jung, *CW* 5, §209.

25. C. G. Jung, *CW* 10, §361.

26. C. G. Jung, "Approaching the Unconscious," *Man and his Symbols* (New York: Doubleday, 1964), p. 98.

27. *Ibid.*, p. 99.

28. James Hillman, "The Bad Mother," *Spring 1983*, p. 171.

29. *Ibid.*, p. 167.

30. *Ibid.*, p. 177.

31. C. G. Jung, *CW* 4, § 728.

32. S. Freud, *The Future of an Illusion*, tr. W.D. Robson-Scott (New York: Doubleday, 1964), p. 88.

33. *Ibid.*, p. 31.

34. By symbol I mean to invoke Jung's definition. For Jung, "Symbols are not signs or allegories for something known; they seek rather to express something that is little known or completely unknown." *CW* 5, §329.

35. "The fateful power of the complex," writes Jung, "comes from the archetype, and this is the real reason why the *consensus gentium* puts a divine or daemonic figure in place of the father. The personal father inevitably embodies the archetype, which is what endows his figure with its fascinating power. The archetype acts as an amplifier, enhancing beyond measure the effects that proceed from the father, so far as these conform to the inherited pattern" (*CW* 4, §744).

36. C. G. Jung, *CW* 4, §729.

37. C. G. Jung, *CW* 7, §216.

38. C. G. Jung, *CW* 7, §214.

39. C. G. Jung, *CW* 9i, §172.

40. C. G. Jung, *CW* 18, §1505.

41. C. G. Jung, *CW* 10, §367.

42. *Ibid.*

43. C. G. Jung, *CW* 10, §511.

GIVING VOICE TO HELL

NOAH PIKES

> Here sighing, and here crying, and loud railing
> Smote on the starless air, with lamentation,
> So that at first I wept to hear such wailing.
>
> Tongues mixed and mingled, horrible execration,
> Shrill shrieks, hoarse groans, fierce yells and
>   hideous blether
> And clapping of hands thereto, without
>   cessation.[1]

I work with persons and their voices, including my own. I call the idea of my practice the "whole voice," as it contains within itself many archetypal oppositions; the sounds and resonances of body/soul, male/female, love/fear, inner/outer, social/imaginal, and the oppositional cluster which forms the focus of this article: light/dark, beauty/ugliness, up/down, good/evil. It is rooted in Alfred Wolfsohn's vision of an unchained human voice, a vision further developed by Roy Hart. Some background to their work is contained in Marita Gunther's article, "On Alfred Wolfsohn," in *Spring 50.* Wolfsohn and Hart both drew inspiration from Jung's work and

Noah Pikes was one of the original members of the Roy Hart Theatre. He now lives in Zürich where he performs and teaches voice.

gave it new significance in the aural dimension, therapeutically and artistically.

Although the "whole voice" is deeply concerned with speech and song, words and music and has strongly influenced some contemporary forms of theater, opera and singing performance, it recognises that institutional or commercial theaters, opera houses and concert halls have increasingly become industries or museums for "culture." Their forms, contents and styles are too concerned with "self-preservation"[2] and are too abstracted and distanced from that superior value of all living organisms that the biologist A. Portmann called "self-representation." Those performance spaces have become the domain of highly trained specialists in speech and song, thereby alienating most other people from these two fundamental realms of the soul and the person. This situation derives from an archetypally based fantasy which distorts our very notion of the person, and the "whole voice" offers a dynamic way of dealing with it.

The "whole voice" has much to do with what French voice specialist J-B. Roche called "the primary level of vocal expression":

> The primary level of vocal expression exists in animals as well as in humans and is perfectly comprehensible and coherent from one ethnic group to another, from one country to another. The secondary level involves learning a verbal language and is thus specifically human, variable and incoherent from one country to another. However, the primary level is never eradicated and it persists through a person's lifetime even though it often has the tendency to minimise itself, taking second place behind a verbal vocal expression.[3]

The voice is a container of the specialised uses we make of it in speech and song, rather than just being a polarised identification with any one single aspect of it. In its search for connections with soul, the "whole voice" work I do proposes a polyphony of voices, each of us not only bass, baritone, tenor, counter-tenor, alto, soprano or mezzo-soprano, but potentially all of these and many more. There are other aspects to the voice than the aesthetic, other gods who give it meaning: the vocal is a unique way into the imaginal. Voice and psyche are linked, far more so than our Judeo-Christian tradition would have us imagine. And the way leads downwards—the link is forged in hell.

Dante tells us from the very moment he arrives at the gate of hell that it is a very noisy place. Once past the gate huge-mouthed Charon roars at him, then Cerberus growls and yells deafeningly. Souls are heard to sigh, wail, weep, cry, yell and howl. Centaurs cry out and shout. Furies shriek loudly. There is uproar and the thunder that greets Dante at the gate continues as a confused roar to the very bottom of the circle of hell. By making his inhabitants raise their voices Dante raises Hell!

Things get more bearable in his *Purgatory* where verbal language in the form of prayer, recitation or speech and music as song, chants and praises predominate, with occasional laughter, tears, shouts or sighs. Heaven is blessed only with speech and infrequent bursts of song. That is, as Dante moves upwards on his soul journey, his writer's imagination moves away from the primary and onto the secondary level of vocal expression. His background fantasy moves from Pan (pandemonium and panic) into Apollo (harmony and philosophical detachment).

"The upward-downward polarity as conceptualised in the matter-spirit opposition, seems to be an archetypal orientation schema basic to the psyche."[4] It is paralleled in the primary level of the human voice. Just listen to your own or other voices in those moments when they move into the primary level—as they do in sighing, yawning, laughing, crying or in sex, or water, or sports crowds—the vertical axis is the central one around which the voice articulates itself.

We conceive of sound as existing in space, as vibrations in a medium. It cannot pass through a vacuum. Yet this space is not only physical—the voice itself is invisible. To talk about it we

often use the language of physical space—it penetrates and ca-
resses, carries and soars, rises and sinks, grows harder or softer,
goes up and down.

A few years ago, I gave some seminars on "Voice & Psyche" at
the Jung Institute in Zürich. Here is one participant's notes on
her first solo journey,on which I accompanied her, into her
"whole voice":

> First at starting note, very shrill and high; everything con-
> stricted, tense, narrow inside (it was my fear; what is he going
> to impose on me, no, I'll make a fool of myself).
> *Then we went down note by note:*
> First I got at ease, I was glad, was feeling stronger, rounder,
> surer, more stable.
> Then 'it' held me from underneath...I had the feeling of some-
> thing sustaining me.
> Then I was flying, with very ample wing movements, slowly,
> smoothly.
> Then I think I saw it slowly flatten, as if I were landing on flat
> ground.
> Then there were big stones...it was quite peaceful.
> Then the sound got 'pointed' like a ray of light which narrows
> and gains in intensity. Then it flattened...like a bow and arrow.
> Then I changed the position of tongue and chin, the sound
> deepened further and went into my belly and I heard my voice
> as if from inside a cavern—my mouth being the cavern, my
> whole body curling inside of my mouth. The cavern got big-
> ger, hollower, darker.
>
> ...my voice was ugly at times, it was hard. From then on to the
> bottom, my voice came from deep down in my belly. At the
> end I heard the dragon at the entrance of the cavern, groaning,
> an ugly hoarse sound getting worse and worse till it stopped
> completely...[5]

Lucienne's voice evoked images, and the images, as you read,
now evoke her voice. In Dante's hell, this power of evocation

("to voice out") gives great strength to his images. The very word recognises the power of the voice on the soul.

In many ancient cultures this recognition was so total that the sound of a person, creature or object was considered to *be* its soul.[6] Many creation myths, such as that of the Egyptian god Thoth or of the Old Testament, tell us that the world was created by a voice, sometimes a sacred word. The magical power of the voice appears in many myths and legends of Northern Europe, (but less so in the South): Thor terrified his enemies in battle with his great voice rising above the tumult, and Lapland was especially celebrated for its magic singers and enchanters. "Enchantment" itself speaks of the power of the voice on the soul.

This is the shamanic way of the voice, and it contrasts strongly with the classical way, with its origins in Greece, continuing through Rome and early Christianity, evolving into the predominantly aesthetic voices of "bel canto," *Lied* and operatic singing. W. B. Stanford describes the ideal Greek voice as "clear, delicate, light, high, melodious and distinctly articulated" and also "steady, clear, raised (but not shrill)." By contrast "hollowness, coarseness, thickness, roughness, breathiness, throatiness and brokenness" were especially disliked, as was a quality described by one writer as "unhewn and full of tree bark."[7]

The shamanic voice embraces these latter qualities and the tree is a sacred shamanic symbol. Eliade tells us that the presence of the helping animal spirits during a shamanic session is manifested by the imitation (by the shaman) of the animal sounds. "The language of the animals" is often the secret language of shamanism, resonating the notion of the primary level of vocal expression. The animal always symbolizes a real and direct link with the beyond.[8]

There seems to be no animal in "bel canto"—originally "buon canto" (good song). Benaroch writes about it that "We think 'clear voice' as we think 'clear mind.'"[9] Another writes, "The

Italian singing voice is Apollonian, by its exteriorised sonorous light: this light recalls its Mediterranean origin, in a way it returns upwards, towards the azure...the body becomes soul, the earth becomes heaven."[10]

So behind the good and beautiful classical voice is an Apollonic fantasy—that same fantasy of spirit which, according to Hillman, says, "Look up, gain distance; there is something beyond and above, and what is above is always and always superior."[11] Physiologically, this ideal classical voice is the search for specific resonances in the upper body, especially in the head—generally in the buccal and nasal cavities, in what is called "the mask." Psychologically, we conceive of ourselves as "persons" (*Personare*: to sound through); the word originated from the external amplifying masks worn by the actors of classical Greek theater. We place the voice as central to our identity, and its orientation is up and out.

The dominant fantasy of Western civilisation has this same orientation, that of ordered surfaces. The christianised persona masked us from ourselves, our bodies, and our voices, and rejected them to the shadows. Hillman's saying that "Christianity cleansed the soul of its polytheistic imaginal possibility"[12] can also be read vocally—our multiple souls with their multiple voices[13] are shaped into mono-tonous loudspeakers. Classical singers spend years developing their "filet de voix" (thread of voice). The Big Bang of creation day ends in the straight clear lines of a whimper.

Students now spend regular sessions at a computer which shows them a visual breakdown of their voice. Their task is to manipulate its resonances in "the mask" so as to correspond to a pre-established pattern of harmonics, seen as bright threads. The aesthetics teacher is now a computer and "good song" is more and more the realm of specialised technicians.

The technicians' inner sense of enchantment when they sing has long since gone—departed with Pan, whose death was announced by a mysterious voice calling out, which provoked a great wailing in the land. "To grasp Pan as nature we must first be grasped by nature, both 'out there' in an empty countryside which speaks in sounds, not words, and 'in here' in a startle reaction."[14] In other words Pan lives in the primary level of vocal expression: in "dells, grottos, water, woods and wilds: never villages, never...the settlements of the civilised: cavern sanctuaries, not constructed temples"[15] of the voice.

My work involves exploring just these kinds of untamed shadow places in the voice—qualities of vocal sound that would not have pleased the Greeks and are considered by contemporary medicine and most voice specialists to be either pathological or potentially damaging to the voice. Under the sway of the Apollonic fantasy, western science does not recognise sources of the voice in the body below the very upper part of the chest, and most singing teachers also follow this line. Yet traditional Vietnamese musical theater, for example, has a number of voices located in specific parts of the middle and lower body.[16]

In going voluntarily into vocal shadows one is led into new body and imaginal resonances. One learns to give voice not only to Pan but to many other gods and archetypal figures. Their sounds may include the rejected Greek ones plus double and chorded sounds, very high pitched whisps or deep wide drones. They are not always pleasant or efficient carriers of words or song, as the Greeks required of their singers, rhetoricians, poets and actors. But the Greeks moved progressively away from the Pan pole towards the Apollonic. Undoubtedly, the kinds of vocal qualities the Greeks idealized were founded in the laws of acoustics governing vocal expression in larger outdoor public spaces. But as angels of atmosphere, as bearers of emotion and feeling, as evocations of other and inhuman realms of the psyche, such shadow sounds are often deeply meaningful to many of the people I work with.

Many of these sounds manifest themselves of their own volition—when experiencing pain, sickness or injury, or even a common cold; or pleasure, as in play, fun, celebration. They come into the voice as cracks, sudden jumps or spaces, thin rasps or breaks, such as one hears in Bill Clinton's voce. Children are especially at home with them. They are the vocal sounds and imaginal places found in the shadow cast by the bright and distant sunlight of Apollo. They belong not only to Pan but also to "The Lord of the Songs of Night." "The Roarer," "the god who is mad," and the god of theater; that is, to Dionysos, (who also has a hidden aspect as Hades).

Antonin Artaud wrote of it this way:

> There are cries of the passions, and in the cry of each passion there are degrees of vibration of the passions; and the world in other times knew a harmonic of the passions. But each illness also has its cry and the form of its death-rattle...And the earthquake has its sound...And from an illness to a passion, from a passion to an earthquake, one can establish some similarities and some strange harmonies of sounds.[17]

Artaud images a fantasy of vocal expression around the Pan-Dionysos pole, which was the basis of his "chthonic music." He describes it as beyond that which we ordinarily call music. This music would be the ensemble of sounds produced by the body, the earth, the elements.[18] He offers a different sense of harmony from the Greco-Chtistian one which we usually imagine as absolute.

Wolfsohn also questioned the significance of the voice after a near-death experience as a soldier in the trenches of World War I. Like a shaman's initiation his experience in hell was the key to new powers of healing and a vision of the human voice that stretched from the classical—he was a discerning opera lover—to the shamanic. "When I speak of singing," he once said, "I view it not only as an artistic exercise but also as a way of knowing oneself." In contrast, Artaud remained rather fixated in his anti-Apollonic stance and one *hears* this in his voice, in the recording he made for radio of "Pour en finir avec le jugement de Dieu."

One hears dryness, rigidity, brittleness, hoarseness and above all a terrible determination.

Wolfsohn showed his students that the human being has a potential vocal range of at least four octaves, and that this can be extended to as many as seven, with time and work (as in Hart's case.) My own voice has a range of around six octaves.[19]The potential variety of textures, colors, and dynamics of a voice is unending.

For Hart this was healing of profound order: "...a biological re-education of the personality through the voice."[20] Compare Hillman's idea that our wounds open doors into soul through its pathologising activity.[21] It is through these same wound doors that many of its voices pass into the world. Body wounds and soul wounds as well as pleasure states have always been the essential sources of man's fantasy and voice, whether in direct expression on the primary level, or in artistic forms implying distancing. Primary and secondary levels interweave as song, chant, poetry, story telling, and theater.

Modernist artists have tended to be more inspired by the pain source than by pleasure, either in their work and its images or in their very lives, or both. Modernists were drawn towards the gate of hell (and rediscovered Dante). Artaud wrote "Fragments of a Journal from Hell," and much of his imagery derives from his vision of the body as hell. Rodin, who made a huge sculptured masterpiece of "The Gate of Hell" "...only knew or cared about Part I of Dante's trilogy. He was not the only 19th century artist to feel that hell 'met his needs as an artist' better than did heaven."[22]

In this respect the individual artist partook of the shamanistic archetype. He tried to remind us that we are also of the earth, of the body and its senses and experiences, and imaginally of the underworld—that through imaging our wounds, through re-presenting their voices, we may also find healing.

Of all the arts, it seems to me that it is the vocal that have remained most under the thumb of Apollo. They keep closed the doors to an authentic artistic expression of our 20th Century wounds. Playwrights, directors and composers often create startling images of the hells under our social and political worlds, or treat deep mythological themes, yet the voices which actually interpret these visions remain unconnected to them. The very sounds of their voices are unconnected to the imaginal realm they try to evoke. Hell is presented by voices from heaven! I suggest that this situation comes partly from the unique place of the voice among all means of human expression, at the very frontier of body and soul. Roy Hart called it "the muscle of the soul' implying that it articulates a soul language.

Through its power of evocation and of enchantment it can be a powerful way back to the imaginal realm of "memoria." But few vocal performers have developed an "imaginal ego."[23] It is not a question of real blood being spent on stage or of "real" screams, but of the re-presentation of raw experience in the light of the imaginal.

As a result, many listen and look elsewhere—to the voices of Black American music, with its shamanic roots still alive; to Afro, to Reggae, to flamenco, to Eastern Europe, India, Inuit, Pygmies, Tibetan monks and whales—anywhere the up *and* down fantasies are represented in the voice; any ways that include some of our other souls, our other wounds, our other persons. Or they listen to music from the down end alone—distorted and deformed—physiologically (Tom Waites, Chet Baker), or electronically (Lauri Anderson, Heavy Metal)—voices from hell are doing good business.

It is to Artaud and Wolfsohn that we owe the first substantial challenges to the fortress of the classical voice. They both pointed to the body as the true source of the voice, moving it down from the head and larynx. In doing so they were telling something that other cultures have known and practised for millennia. Wolfsohn, unlike Artaud, made no journeys to exotic places—he rediscovered voice in a setting deeply symbolic of the hell of early 20th Century Europe (while lying on a pile of bodies of moaning soldiers left for dead in World War I). He never studied vocal techniques from other lands. Nevertheless his work has opened up vocal doors that echo through the halls of the collective unconscious.

From the point of view of the heroic ego, the body is a hell of a problem. It has animal urges, rhythms, energies and sounds, and an inevitable disintegration in death. The Christian conclusion, after Augustine, was that to be born into a body was to be automatically born into sin, estranged from God. In this hell the Devil replied, according to William Blake:

> Man has no Body distinct from his Soul.
> Energy is the only life and is from the Body.
> Energy is Eternal Delight.[24]

The Church, said Blake, sees bodily energy as the Devil. Thus the body's voices have always been considered diabolic. The early Church knew the power of the voice on the soul. Augustine even had hesitations about the use of singing.[25] Its use has been strictly controlled and mostly put into the care of specialists.

Since the death of Pan, the march "upwards" of civilization has required Western man to put the voices of his inner animals and monsters, his passions and sicknesses, even of the four elements within himself, into the shadows.

Greek mythology's rejection of the wounded Body/Soul, of the shamanic source of the voice, is reflected in the near absence of the primary level expression in its visual and verbal images. There is no special voice or breath as the source of creation. Orpheus, the one most closely linked with the shamanic archetype, while keeping the power over nature through his voice, is given only beautiful sound and a lyre, and fails to use his voice at the crucial moment with Euridyce. Pan pipes clear tones, yet even so, in the form of Marsyas he suffers a terrible defeat in the musical contest against Apollo. The Underworld is virtually silent apart from the occasional Cerberus bark. Even Pan and Diony-sos are rarely to be seen with open mouths. Actaeon, devoured by his own hounds, seems to utter no cries—his dogs however, have wide open mouths.[26] In general only animals, monsters and oracles have been given a voice on the primary level—the persons play instruments, sing sweetly or speak words. It is as if, for the Greeks, the act of mythological representation in writing, painting or sculpture was only *possible* through Apollonic eyes. (They were, after all, *his* arts.) This distancing of humans from the natural world was to develop much further in the monotheistic civilizations of Judaism and Christianity. Animals became "only animals," only there for man's domination and use.

Yet the voices of our souls call out from the shadows and in certain moments take over from our civilised voices—in crowds, emotional states, sexual excitememt, in neuroses and psychoses,[27] in violent acts, and sometimes even in sleep,[28] or when awakening, shouting, crying or gasping from (Pan's) nightmare. In such moments the unconscious feels the attraction of the "down" pole, as the devil raises his voice and we give voice to hell. We become hellcats or hellhounds, making a hell of a noise, giving others hell, having "a hell of a good time," doing it "for the hell of it."

We are ambiguous about hell as we are about the body, and our language expresses this—"hell" is used as an intensifier for both pleasure and pain; adding spice to verbal imagery. The word itself is part of a whole etymological cluster including hall, hole, hollow, hulk, and hold (of a ship) as well as cell and occult; the Indo-European root being "Kel"—to hide. Hell as the hidden under/world of the body as viewed by the head. Viewed thus, and essentially as belly, there comes another cluster: bell, and to bell (stag voices), bellow, blow, bellows, and belch are all etymologically connected, while below, bowel, vowel and howl are connected on the sound image level.[29]

In some non-Western cultures this lower place, physically and imaginally, is recognised as the true center of human being and an essential center for the voice. But Western civilization, in following the attraction of the upward fantasy, puts the center in the head. Those who are not centered there, "who have lost the good of intellect," become inhabitants of Dante's hell, which is also "a wide throat."

An essential function of the artist is just this reminding us of the other pole, where the shadows live. "It is the opposite which is good for us" (Heraclitus. Frag 46.) In seeking the "Mariage of Heaven & Hell" Blake sought to heal the deepest wound of all—the unconscious fixation, on the collective and personal level, with one pole only. He recognised, and showed, that the gate of hell is also a gate of the imaginal—perhaps *the* gate. He made sublime art from his visions of the body re-membered; a self-presentation of the soul. When this gate is unrecognised through some form of contained representation, of disciplined imaging, which we call art, the quality of what passes through it, compelled by the impulse for self-presentation, becomes a literal acting out of hell.

Then the soul needs not only to act out its images in hellish behaviours—rape, torture, war, terrorism, abuse—it seems to need almost as much to *hear* them, in screams, yells, cries and moans. Turn off the sound when watching such behaviours in movies and something essential is missing. Such movies try to become ever more "realistic," but the cathartic process doesn't work without accompanying sound.

The body's search for the soul,[30] in the form of the lost realm of the imaginal, becomes the search for the abandoned child, in the form of its voice, "which is always there, and must be there as an archetypal necessity."[31] *It* is the one out there who is raising hell.

The alternative to the literal acting out of hell would be the recognition of its psychological necessity in its "coniunctio" with heaven, in the manner of artistic representation. Through the work of the "whole voice" a new and dynamic way has been opened up whereby this necessity may be re-called and enacted imaginally. Its point of departure is just this acceptance, vocally and psychically of what is there, in the whole of the voice, beyond any aesthetic models that culture would impose upon it. We call it "sticking to the voice."

The actor, like the singer, had also been held for some twenty-four centuries in the fantasy of the "beautiful voice."[32] Otto describes him as "the most recent descendant of the spirit of the dual being who is Dionysos,"[33] yet Artaud despaired of him: "...of all Europeans, especially the actor no longer knows how to cry out; his throat has become a monstrous abstraction which only knows how to speak!"[34] Western actors and singers of the classical school have lost their connection to their ancestors, the shamans, to their own breath sounds, to their own "hara" (Japanese belly center) and to their own hell.

The "beautiful voice" remains entrenched as *the* aesthetic summit, not only in music and theater but also in the medical and therapeutic professions concerned with the vocal and speech "apparatus." As with our multiple souls, our multiple voices are relegated to the pathological, or at best, to the level of oddities or curiosities. The imaginal ground of the voice is ignored or simply unknown. Its retrieval implies reparation of the artificial separation that the classical voice has also made between the clear bright sound and that of the breath alone, carrying little or no vocal sound with it. You hear it when sighing, yawning or whispering and it is a basic and expressive part of our primal vocal world. It has been judged as not beautiful and not useful, although it is the very life energy of the voice itself. We recognise its importance, however, in the double sense of the word "atmosphere" (breath-sphere). One meaning of psyche originally was "breath." In including the breath sound as an integral part of the voice—for the hell of it—we return psyche to voice and give it atmosphere.

NOTES

1. Dante Alighieri, "Hell," *The Divine Comedy*, tr. D. Sayers (London, 1949), pp. 85-86.

2. Adolf Portmann, "Color Symbolism," *Eranos Yearbook 1974*.

3. J-B. Roche, "La Voix de l'Enfant," *Le Journal d'Audiophonologie* (Besançon, 1980). My translation, p. 23.

4. James Hillman, "Parapsychology," *Loose Ends* (Dallas: Spring Publications, 1978), p. 134.

5. L. Margerat. Private communication, 1989.

6. See the discussion on "Primitive Music" by various authors in *The New Oxford History of Music*, Vol. I. (Oxford: Oxford University Press, 1957).

7. W. B. Stanford, *The Sound of Greek* (Berkeley, California: University of California Press, 1967), pp. 148-50.

8. Mircea Eliade, *Le Chananisme* (Paris, 1951). See discussion on shamanism, animal spirits, and their voices, pp. 93-102.

9. M. Benaroche, *De l'art vocal* (Biarritz, 1958). My translation.

10. J. & B. Ott, *La Pédagogie de la Voiz et les Techniques Européenes du Chant*, (Issy les Moulineaux. No date). My translation.

11. James Hillman, *Re-visioning Psychology* (New York: Harper & Row, 1977), p. 69.

12. James Hillman, "Abandoning the Child," *Loose Ends* (Dallas: Spring Publications, 1978), p. 17.

13. Hillman, "Parapsychology," *Loose Ends*, p. 128.

14. James Hillman, *Pan & the Nightmare* (Dallas: Spring Publications, 1979), p. xxi.

15. *Ibid.*

16. Q. H. Tran, *"Les Musiques Vocales,"* *L'Espirit des Voix* (Grenoble, 1990), p. 48.

17. Antin Artaud, *"Les Tarahumaras,"* (Isère, 1955), p. 193.

18. Antin Artaud, *Oeuvres Complètes*, Vol. 7 (Paris, 1970). My translation. See the discussion on Artaud's ideas about music in Florence de Mèredieu, "La Pensée Émet des Signes, le Corps Émet des Sons," in *Traverses No. 20* (Paris, 1980), the Revue of the Centre national d'art et culture Georges Pompidou.

19. R. Luchsinger, *International Journal of Phoniatry*, Vol. 8, No. 4., 1956. A leading Swiss voice specialist examined the voice of one of Wolfsohn's students and found her to possess a vocal range of 5 octaves and 6 tones.

20. Roy Hart from part of a spoken introduction to a demonstration recording, 1967.

21. Hillman, *Re-Visioning*, p. 67.

22. F.V. Grunfeld, *Rodin* (London, 1987), p. 176.

23. See Hillman's discussion of "memoria" and the "imaginal ego" in Part 2 of *The Myth of Analysis* (New York: Harper & Collins, 1972), especially pp. 180-181.

24. William Blake, *The Marriage of Heaven & Hell* (Oxford: Oxford University Press, 1974).

25. Significantly "sin" in Middle English had the form "singen."

26. The stone frieze is from a temple to E. Selinus, in the National Museum, Palermo, Italy.

27. See P. J. Moses, *The Voice of Neurosis* (New York, 1954).

28. L. A. MacNeilage, *Activity of Speech Apparatus during Sleep and its relation to Dream Reports,* (Doctoral dissertation, Columbia University, 1974).

29. See Paul Kugler, *Alchemy of Discourse* (London: Bucknell University Press, 1980), for an extensive discussion of verbal sound and image: "On a deep level (unconscious) the meaning relation between the complex of phonetically associated words is via the archetypal image."

30. Oscar Wilde somewhere describes hell as either a soul without a body or a body without a soul.

31. *Pan & the Nightmare, ibid.*

32. J. Martin, *Voice in Modern Theater* (London, 1991), discusses this history and continues with sources and aspects of the emergence of "a new rhetoric." The author pays homage to the Roy Hart Theater's influence, saying that "...its effects have been felt not just in group Theater Movement, but also in the whole approach to the voice as a means of communication.", p. 69.

33. W. F. Otto, *Dionysos: Myth & Cult* (Blomington, Indiana: University of Indiana Press, 1965), p. 210.

34. Artaud, *Oeuvres Complètes,* Vol. 4 (Paris, 1970), p. 163.

MAX NORDAU'S *DEGENERATION,* C.G. JUNG'S TAINT

RICHARD NOLL

THE DEGENERATE'S PRAYER

Have pity upon us, good Lord, because we do the things we ought not to do, and we do not the things we ought to do – and there is no health in us. But Thou, O Lord, knowest that we are the tainted offspring of forefathers beggared in their bodies by luxury and riotous living, and of fathers who sapped their manhood in vice. Pardon our murders, our brutalities, our thefts, our crimes of cunning and cruelty, which we daily commit. Put sorrow and penitence in our hearts. Forgive our fellow men, who have helped to cripple our childhood and who now torture us and curse us—for they are blind. Teach them how to be just to us, for Thou, O Lord, knowest the heart of man. Our hope is in Thee for justice, and our trust for mercy.[1]

Nineteen ninety-five will mark the centenary of the appearance of Max Nordau's *Degeneration* in its English translation. Indeed, throughout 1895 the newspapers and popular journals were filled with two compelling stories: the controversy over Nordau, and Oscar Wilde's sodomy trial. The

Richard Noll, Ph.D., teaches in the Department of Psychology, West Chester University, West Chester, PA.

publication of *Degeneration* was no small event in the English-speaking world of the Yellow Nineties, as it drove a stake into the heart of each average 19th-century individual who secretly feared another's discovery of hereditary taint in one's own blood. The medical theory of hereditary degeneration haunted millions in *fin-de-siécle* Europe. "Outing" tainted individuals became a brutal social pastime. Revelations of taint could lead to *Berufsverbot*—being shut out of one's choice of vocation. This was not lost on C.G. Jung (1875-1961), a young medical student in Basel, Switzerland, when the cultural storm over *Degeneration* swept Central Europe. Nordau claimed hereditary degeneration was endemic in Europe; Jung could see it in his own family.

Max Nordau: Nastiness as an Art Form

The shock of the brilliant, unrelenting prose of *Degeneration* made Max Nordau one of the most famous men of the 1890s, although he is undeservedly forgotten now. Let us then review the details of this remarkable man's life.

Max Nordau (1849-1923) was born in Pest, Hungary, the son of an Orthodox Jewish rabbi. Although in later adulthood he would be regarded as an icon of 19th-century bourgeois tradition and liberal rationality, he apparently found his own strict religious environment repugnant and violently rejected his roots. As a young man he left Pest and his family, and in a nominal *enantiodromia* changed even his identity from his birth name, Simon Maximilian Südfeld, to Max Nordau; that is, from "southern field" to "northern meadow." He eventually settled in Paris, that cauldron of *fin-de-siécle* culture, and gained fame in the early 1880s as a journalist, social critic, novelist, Liberal, and *aliéniste*, having trained under Charcot at the Salpêtrière asylum for mad women. The rotund polyglot Dr. Nordau became an atheist, a fervent Darwinian, and a proselytizer of scientism. He was noted for his formidable intellect and clear prose and was remarkably well-read in the literature, philosophy and science of his day. His

polemics were therefore well-founded yet viscious, often com-
bining insightful criticism with petty spleen-venting in that typical 19th century mode.

In the late 1890s he became a Zionist, second in importance in
the Zionist movement to Theodore Herzl, a fellow Hungarian
Jew from Pest. He was among the first proponents of
"Reconstructionist Zionism" which promoted the return to a
homeland founded on secular Jewish culture rather than theo-
cratic principles. Hence, like Sigmund Freud, Nordau, too, was
"a godless Jew."

Nordau vigorously opposed Herzl's initial plan to establish a
Jewish homeland in Uganda when Palestine seemed out of the
question. In an ironic twist of fate, Nordau survived an assassina-
tion attempt on 19 December 1903 at a Hanukkah ball in Paris
by a confused young Zionist student who cried out, "Death to
Nordau, the East African!", before firing two off-target shots
that wounded a bystander. According to Alex Bein, Herzl's
biographer, after the shots were fired, "A panic ensued, in the
midst of which Nordau alone remained calm."[2]

Max Nordau, as far as we know, never met C.G. Jung, even
though their lives were linked, curiously, by the Zionist movement. Jung's maternal grandfather, Samuel Prieswerk (1799-
1871) was a prominent Protestant minister in Basel and a professor of Hebraic studies. He founded a group of Swiss Protestant
fundamentalists who sought the fulfillment of Biblical prophecy
through supporting the proto-Zionist movement's cause for the
return of the Jews to Palestine. For this reason, the First International Zionist Congress was held in Basel in 1897. The 22 year-
old medical student Jung could have conceivably met the famous
Max Nordau during this time.

Although his initial fame came from his sharply worded,
trenchant, indeed *nasty*, journalistic pieces of social criticism, it
was a book-length exercise in atheistic nastiness entitled *Conventional Lies of Civilization* (1883) that created his notoriety. Dr.
Nordau's prediction in the "Preface" to his first edition that,

"the author knows that many people will hold up their hands in holy horror when they read it" was an accurate one. This book was banned, confiscated and burned in Austria-Hungary after the Imperial Council of Vienna condemned it for such sins as "the Crime of insulting a church and sect recognized by the State"; the "Crime of insulting the members of the imperial family"; the "Crime of denouncing Religion"; and the "Crime of disturbing the public peace by attempting to arouse contempt or hatred for the person of the Emperor."[3] This last "crime" may indeed be said to be the archetypal sin of any iconoclast who dares to question the "myth" of any "great man."

No doubt intrigued by the confiscation and burning of the books of this secular Jewish physician in his home country, the 29 year-old Viennese neurologist Sigmund Freud called on Dr. Nordau in Paris in 1885. Freud was in Paris at that time studying under Nordau's teacher and subsequent colleague, Charcot, to gain expertise in the specialty of nervous and mental diseases. As Ernest Jones tells it, "He called on Max Nordau with a letter of introduction, but he found him vain and stupid and did not cultivate his acquaintance"[4]—an unsurprising reaction indeed from the young man who was later to become perhaps *the* leading prophet of 20th-century modernity.

Nordau's circle of contacts was quite extensive, from Theodore Herzl (1860-1904) to J.M. Charcot (1825-1893) to Cesare Lombroso (1836-1909) to Arminius Vambéry (1832-1913), the great Hungarian scholar, ethnographer, and linguist. Vambéry still retains a certain fame in his country of origin as the Hungarian counterpart to England's rogue scholar, linguist, and explorer Sir Richard Burton, and indeed was even depicted on a postage stamp in Hungary in the 1950s. Bram Stoker met him several times in England and refers to him in *Dracula* (1897).[5] It is thought that Stoker based the character of Prof. Dr. Van Helsing on Vambéry.[6]

Dracula himself is the consummate *fin-de-siécle* cultural horror: something living hundreds of years yet dead, something dead but undead, draining the vitality of the living, like European civilization itself. Dracula is the consummate degenerate. In Chapter 25 of Stoker's *Dracula*, Dr. Van Helsing uses descriptions from the eminent Italian alienist and criminologist, Cesare Lombroso, to describe Dracula's essence to Minna Harker, who then, while in a somnambulistic trance, repeats back to Van Helsing: "The Count is a criminal type. Nordau and Lombroso would so classify him, and *qua* criminal he is of imperfectly formed mind."[7] Such was the fame of Max Nordau and his *Degeneration*.

In the 19th century "genius" and "degeneration" were linked. Nordau made much of the "mad genius" idea in *Degeneration*. When told by a journalist friend in Paris in September 1895 that Nordau used him as a prime example in *Degeneration* to back up his argument that many men of genius are degenerates, Oscar Wilde could respond, "I quite agree with Dr. Nordau's assertion that all men of genius are insane, but Dr. Nordau forgets that all sane people are idiots."[8] Yet, by July 1896, writing to the British Home Secretary from his dismal cell in Reading Prison, Wilde would instead plead for early release by arguing he was "rightly found guilty...(of) forms of sexual madness...diseases to be cured by a physician, rather than crimes to be punished by a judge. In the works of eminent men of science such as Lombroso and Nordau...this is especially insisted on with reference to the intimate connection between madness and the literary and artistic temperament..." Wilde then refers to Nordau's references to him in *Degeneration* "as a specially typical example of this fatal law."[9]

Degeneration

Max Nordau tells us in his famous apocalyptic book of 1892, *Entartung* (the translation entitled *Degeneration* appeared in 1895),[10] that the fashionable late 19th-century phrase *fin de siécle* "is a name covering both what is characteristic of many modern phenomena, and also the underlying mood which in them finds expression."[11] The "modern phenomena" he had in mind could be found in late 19th-century "degenerate" movements in art (e.g., Symbolism), literature (Tolstoism, Symbolism, Naturalism, Realism), music ("the Richard Wagner Cult," as Nordau refers to it) and philosophy (Schopenhauer, Nietzsche, von Hartmann, Blavatsky, et al.). *Degeneration* is a massive diagnostic assessment of *fin-de-siécle* culture. Had Freud's "psychoanalysis" or Jung's "analytical psychology" existed in 1892, they, too, would have been skewered by Nordau as cults invented by degenerate geniuses for less gifted degenerates whose judgment was organically impaired. This is how "Mad Max" Nordau sees it:

> The proposition which I set myself to prove may now be taken as demonstrated. In the civilized world there obviously prevails a twilight mood which finds expression, amongst other ways, in all sorts of odd aesthetic fashions. All these new tendencies, realism or naturalism, 'decadentism,' neo-mysticism, and their subvarieties, are manifestations of degeneration and hysteria, and identical with the mental stigmata which the observations of the clinicists have unquestionably established as belonging to these. But both degeneration and hysteria are the consequences of the excessive organic wear and tear suffered by the nations through the immense demands on their activity, and through the rank growth of large towns.[12]

"Dr. Max Nordau has by his book *Degeneration* produced no small sensation throughout the world," admits an anonymous reviewer in a volume which appeared in 1896 under the title *Regeneration: A Reply to Max Nordau.*[13] Nordau's assertion that hereditary degeneration had progressed to the point where it tainted persons at all levels of European culture offended many (especially those in the arts), but *terrified* many more. "It is no wonder that his work has become as it were a nightmare to millions of minds," observes this same critic.[14]

George Bernard Shaw was the first prominent critic of Nordau's *Degeneration* after it appeared in English in February 1895 (going through no less than seven reprintings in that year alone), and in that same year he published a scathing rebuttal in the journal *Liberty*. Shaw's critique was then later published in book form under the title *The Sanity of Art: An Exposure of the Current Nonsense about Artists Being Degenerate*.[15] To his other major critics, it was Nordau himself who was "mad." "Degeneration constitutes Nordau. He is himself an abnormality and pathological type," claimed Nicholas Murray Butler, Professor of Philosophy and Education at Columbia College in New York, in 1896.[16]

In his nasty, "A Reply to My Critics," published in the widely read journal, *The Century*, in the autumn of 1895, Nordau instead launched an early counterattack:

> Truth to tell, I have not been able to keep pace with my critics to date. I have found among twenty critics one who had anything to teach me [Nordau probably means Shaw], while the other nineteen indulged in mere foolish abuse...I had theoretically anticipated that they were capable of strongly stimulating the intellect, making it inventive, inspiring new similes and unprecedented imprecations. But, strange to say, in the case of my assailants this anticipation has not been verified. They invent nothing. The substance of their brains seems to be lead or clay...They content themselves with gnashing their teeth, rolling their eyes, clenching their fists, and emitting guttural cries. An excited Hottentot would do exactly the same. What can one do with such antagonists? The best thing to do, perhaps, would be to perpetuate their savage attitudes by means of instantaneous photography, and put them all together in an album of grotesque caricatures.[17]

Perhaps the most cutting insult of all to Nordau was to turn the treatment table on *him:*

> In persons of a low stage of intellectual development the power of repartee, as is well known, is limited to the observa-

tion, "You're another!" That was the happy inspiration that seized all my critical antagonists...They assured their readers I was myself a degenerate, a lunatic. Some went even further...They hinted they might from my family history deduce the proof that I was not only myself a madman, but that I was descended from insane ancestors.[18]

Concern over "insane ancestors" was precisely the preoccupation of the young Dr. Jung—with no small help from the cultural hysteria caused by eminent Dr. Nordau in *fin-de-siècle* Europe.

Jung's Hereditarian Concerns

Due to the work of the eminent French *aliénistes* Benedict Augustin Morel and Valentin Magnan, theories of hereditary degeneration dominated medical education in the late 19th century.[19] Max Nordau brought it to its exaltation in popular culture. Degeneracy was literally thought to be transmitted in the protoplasm of the sperm of the father to his progeny, and the physical and mental stigmata of degeneration were thought to worsen with each new generation leading to idiocy, further vegetation, and eventually death until the family line died out. Although the progression of degeneracy within an individual and therefore within a family could be halted through "therapeutics" (e.g., halting substance abuse, moving away from cramped urban centers, etc.), the weakness was still passed on to the next generation. Thus, the theory of degeneration has been called, and rightly so, "the Christian notion of original sin embodied in the nervous system,"[20] and it obsessed persons at all levels of society at the turn of the century—including C.G. Jung, who matured and underwent medical training in this potent *fin-de-siécle* milieu.

Jung's earliest psychiatric publications make reference to degeneration theory until about 1906, after which the non-hereditarian psychoanalytic concepts of Freud predominate. Jung even mentions the work of Nordau, with whom he agrees in principle, in his 1905 essay on "Cryptomnesia," but distances himself from Nordau's extremism and "pseudo-psychiatric witch-hunting."[21] All those working under the successive leadership of August Forel and Eugen Bleuler at the Burghölzli in Zürich at the turn of the century had to remain abstinent from alcohol, for the physicians at the Burghölzli were the soldiers fighting in the front lines in the war against degeneration. *Civilization could be saved by changes in their own private behavior, for only then could they heal their degenerate patients.* The two most prevalent populations at the Burghölzli in 1900 (Jung arrived in December of that year) were degenerative disorders: dementia praecox and alcoholism. Jung lived in an apartment at the Burghölzli until early 1909. He was immersed in a sea of degeneracy twenty-four hours a day.

At first, these institutionalized individuals must have been difficult for Jung to face without fear, for according to the dominant medical philosophy of his day, Jung was tainted in spades: Jung's mother had bouts of mental illness; his father was a "weak character"; his cousin, a spiritualist medium, was nonetheless an "hysteric" and the subject of his first published clinical case study;[22] Jung himself was bad seed and suffered from hysterical fainting fits as a child. As a man he feared that his "confrontation with the unconscious" may have been the prodromal phase of a lifelong degenerative Nietzschean psychosis.[23] If some of the psychiatric authorities of his day (including Nordau) could claim Jesus was nothing more than a psychotic who suffered from hallucinations and grandiose delusions,[24] then Jung's own deification experience[25] would certainly nail *him* to the cross in due time and seal his eventual fate in an asylum.

Jung's fear of his own hereditary taint may have been an unspoken motivation for his sudden choice of psychiatry as a career, and indeed a curious, seemingly paranoid, confession in *Memories, Dreams, Reflections* bears this out. When first begin-

ning his psychiatric career at the Burghölzli he tells us, "I secretly compiled statistics on the hereditary background of my
Swiss colleagues" in order to understand "the psychiatric mental-
ity."[26] This statement no longer seems so paranoid to the modern reader when it is realized that Jung was trying to gauge how
progressively degenerate he was in comparison to his fellow al-
ienists, who were perhaps also attracted to their profession
through a curiosity about their own morbidity.

Jung's personal library (catalogued after his death)[27] contains
the two volume 1896 German edition of *Entartung* as well as the
1883 German edition of *Conventional Lies*. Both volumes were
probably purchased and read during his medical school days,
and therefore Jung may have been aware of the eminent Max
Nordau's claim that, "The degenerate and the insane are the
predestined disciples of Schopenhauer and (Eduard) von Hartmann,"[28] two philosophers who, along with the (eventual)
madman Nietzsche, had a profound influence on Jung during his
student years.

Statistics were often compiled and published on the heredity of
"degenerates" and "geniuses" alike at the turn of the century.
Therefore, by collecting such hereditarian data on his psychiatric colleagues, Jung was following the standard scientific research
methodology of his era. Jung's famous Basel grandfather, C.G.
Jung the Elder, and his apocryphal blood-tie to Goethe[29] were
the fruits of genius on his own family tree. But which was he,
degenerate or genius? Jung's choice of psychiatry as a vocation
gave him the tools with which he could determine his true nature. The *persona medici* was also a safe haven from accusations
of taint.

Jung eventually resolved his concern with degeneration. In
September 1909, on his way to America, Jung broke his vow of
abstinence to Eugen Bleuler, his Chief at the Burghölzli, by shar-
ing wine with Freud. This simple, symbolic act not only her-
alded his new, whole-hearted allegiance to Freud and psychoanalysis but was also his rejection of Bleuler and degeneration

theory in psychiatry. Only then did Jung begin to seek a way to reverse the notion of hereditary taint—his and ours. How Jung cultivated a path of renewal and redemption for himself and others is a story best told another time.

NOTES

1. This "prayer" appears in Albert Wilson, *Unfinished Man* (London: Greening and Co., Ltd., 1910). It is reproduced from the citation in Richard Walter, "What Became of the Degenerate? A Brief History of a Concept," *Journal of the History of Medicine and Allied Sciences,* 11 (1956), p. 422.

2. Alex Bein, *Theodore Herzl: A Biography* (Philadelphia: Jewish Publication Society of America, 1940), pp. 485-486.

3. Max Nordau, "Preface to the Sixth Edition," *The Conventional Lies of Our Civilization* (London: William Heineman, 1895).

4. Ernest Jones, *The Life and Work of Sigmund Freud,* Vol. I (New York: Basic Books, 1953), p. 188.

5. Bram Stoker, *Dracula* (London: Constance, 1897).

6. For an account of Vambéry's magnetic personality, see Max Nordau, "My Recollections of Vambéry," in Arminius Vambéry, *The Life and Adventures of Arminius Vambéry, Written By Himself* (New York: Frederick A. Stokes, Co., 1914), pp. xv-xxiv.

7. *The Essential Dracula: The Definitive Annotated Edition of Bram Stoker's Classic Novel,* ed. Leonard Wolf (New York: Plume, 1993), p. 403. For additional details concerning the use of 19th century psychiatric thought by Stoker in *Dracula,* see Richard Noll, *Vampires, Werewolves, and Demons: Twentieth Century Reports in the Psychiatric Literature* (New York: Brunner/Maazel, 1992), pp. 9-19.

8. Richard Ellman, *Oscar Wilde* (New York: Alfred Knopf, 1987), p. 550.

9. Karl Beckson, *London in the 1890s: A Cultural History* (New York: W. W. Norton, 1992), p. 65.

10. Max Nordau, *Entartung* (Berlin: C. Dunker, 1892). All citations from this remarkable work are from the first English edition of *Degeneration* (New York and London: D. Appleton, 1895). Important as this book was, it was only read for a generation or so. By 1914 the "moderns" had won the cultural war and 19th century bourgeois moralists like Nordau were pushed aside. The last German and French editions appeared in 1909. A second English edition appeared in 1912, and the last Italian edition appeared in 1925. A 1966 reprint of the first English edition appeared in 1966 with a useful introduction by historian George Mosse.

11. Nordau, *Degeneration*, p. 1.

12. Nordau, *Degeneration*, p. 43.

13. [Anonymous], *Regeneration: A Reply to Max Nordau* (New York: G.P. Putnam's Sons, 1896), p. 9. This book was later revealed to have been the work of the British critic Alfred Egmont Hake.

14. [Anonymous], *Regeneration*, p. 9.

15. George Bernard Shaw, *The Sanity of Art: An Exposure of the Current Nonsense about Artists Being Degenerate* (London: 1908).

16. N. M. Butler, "Introduction," in [Anonymous], *Regeneration*, p. ix.

17. Max Nordau, "A Reply to My Critics," *The Century*, no. 28 (1895), p. 546.

18. *Ibid.*

19. For excellent scholarly surveys of the dominance of degeneration theory in the 19th century, see *Degeneration: The Dark Side of Progress*, eds. J. Edward Chamberlin and Sander Gilman (New York: Columbia University Press, 1985); Daniel Pick, *Faces of Degeneration: A European Disorder, c. 1848-1918* (Cambridge: Cambridge University Press, 1989); and Ian Dowbiggin, *Inheriting Madness: Professionalization and Psychiatric Knowledge in 19th Century France* (Berkeley: University of California Press, 1991).

20. George Drinka, *The Birth of Neurosis: Myth, Malady and the Victorians* (New York: Simon and Schuster, 1984), p. 53.

21. C.G. Jung, "Cryptomnesia" (1905), *CW* 1, §175.

22. The publication of Jung's dissertation in 1902 and its medical case history of "S.W." (his mediumistic cousin Helene) stigmatized his mother's side of the family (the Prieswerks) in the small community of Basel. Everyone knew the Jungs and the Prieswerks and knew about the seances Jung held with his mother and female Prieswerk cousins. "In those days considerable stress was put on heredity, and the whole maternal side of the family appeared to be tainted with insanity. Rumors circulated that the younger Prieswerk daughters could not find husbands because of Jung's dissertation and that Helene had died from a broken heart. Actually, she died from tuberculosis." Henri Ellenberger, "Carl Gustav Jung: His Historical Setting," in Hertha Riese (ed.), *Historical Explorations in Medicine and Psychiatry* (New York: Springer, 1978), p. 149.

23. See James Hillman, "Dionysus in Jung's Writings," *Spring 1972* (New York).

24. There is no better introduction to the *fin de siécle* debate on this issue than Albert Schweitzer's doctoral dissertation, originally published in German in 1913, the year of Jung's deification experience. See Albert Schweitzer, *The Psychiatric Study of Jesus: Exposition and Criticism*, tr. and intr. Charles Joy (Boston: Beacon, 1948).

25. Jung's visionary deification experience is detailed in Richard Noll, "Jung the *Leontocephalus*," *Spring 53* (Putnam, Connecticut, 1992).

26. C.G. Jung, *Memories, Dreams, Reflections* (New York: Pantheon, 1962), pp. 112-113.

27. See *C.G. Jung Bibliothek: Katalog* (Küsnacht-Zürich, 1967).

28. Nordau, *Degeneration*, p. 20.

29. For Jung's supposed kinship with Goethe, see *Memories, Dreams, Reflections*, p. 35.

WHICH WAY I FLY IS HELL:
DIVINATION AND THE SHADOW
OF THE WEST

STEPHEN KARCHER

L ucifer's realization in Milton's *Paradise Lost*—"Which way I fly is Hell: myself am Hell"[1]—could be a motto for the modern world. Freud began his ground-breaking *Interpretation of Dreams* with the Vergilian prefix: *Flectere si nequo superos Acheronta movebo/* "If I cannot bend the Gods on high, I will at least set Acheron in uproar." Marx's revolutionary book, *Das Kapital*, put the underworld slums of industrial London at the center of political thought. Picasso's shocking painting, *Les demoiselles d'Avignon*, offered a demonic brothel filled with savage masks as the locus of beauty. And Rimbaud's hallucinatory *Un saison en enfer* proposed a poetic that loosed the caged voices of desire through a "systematic derangement of all the senses."[2] Western culture, ever in search of some new vision, has been irresistibly drawn into what Jung called the Shadow.

The dream of a European theologian cited by Jung in 1934 is paradigmatic of this culture at the brink:

> [I] dreamed that I saw on a mountain a kind of Castle of the Grail. [I] went along a road that seemed to lead straight to the

Stephen Karcher is co-director of the Eranos Yi Ching Project in Ascona, Switzerland, and editor of *The Yi Ching and the Ethic of the Image*.

foot of the mountain and up it. But as [I] drew near [I] discovered...that a chasm separated [me] from the mountain, a deep
darksome gorge with underworldly water rushing along the
bottom. A steep path led downwards...[3]

"This water is no figure of speech," Jung observed, "but a living symbol of the dark psyche (*CW* 9i, §33)... earthy and tangi-
ble, it is also the fluid of the instinct-driven body, blood and the
flowing of blood, the odor of the beast, carnality heavy with
passion" (*CW* 9i, §41).

But Jung saw a drive in this breakdown. In 1928, writing on
"The Spiritual Problem of Modern Man, " he maintained:

> Our age wants to experience the psyche for itself. It wants
> original experience and not assumptions. How else can we ex-
> plain this zeal, this almost fanatical worship of everything un-
> savory? It is because these things ... are of the substance of the
> psyche and therefore as precious as fragments of manuscripts
> salvaged from ancient middens...[The] crux of the spiritual
> problem today is to be found in the fascination which the
> psyche holds for modern man...[it] touches those irrational
> and—as history shows—incalculable psychic forces which
> transform the life of peoples and civilizations in ways that are
> unforeseen and unforeseeable.
>
>

CW 10, §173; 177; 191

If, for Jung, the drive of our time is to experience the underworld of the psyche, the task imposed upon us is the awareness
this experience brings—the "psychic connection." For it is in the
fluid, dark interior world where blood, thought and image mix
that any change takes place.

But how to approach this "Shadow of the West" if one lives in
the Western world itself?

The *Yi Ching*, the ancient Chinese Book of Oracles, enters
modern culture through just this Luciferian "nick" in the hierar-
chy of values. It strikes people first as "superstition" and, if they
look behind their rational condescension, as shadow, psyche,

blood-soul, fate: in other words, as a pagan, magical world. For those who use it, however, divination with the *Yi Ching* is not exoticism or chicanery but a "sign that we are beginning to relate to the alien elements in ourselves" (*CW* 13, § 72). It turns us away from "thought" which is normative and communal into the underworld of dream and psychic image—what the ancients called the Kingdom of Hades. It involves us with the demons or *daimones*, the underworld images which are "living units of the unconscious psyche"—those "architects of dreams and symptoms" (*CW* 8, § 210) usually only spoken about from a safe psychological perspective.

Pagans and Christians

But the demons have another, very conflicted, context.[4] The Late Latin shift in the meaning of the word "daimon" from "spirit or genius" to "evil spirit, demon, devil" marks the end of the Antique World, a border that is psychological as well as historical. Though the Dionysian processions, the chthonic Mysteries and the theriomorphic representations of the Gods have vanished, "all our lives we possess, side by side with our...directed and adapted thinking, a fantasy-thinking which corresponds to this antique state of mind" (*CW* 5, §36). This "fantasy-thinking" produces "a world picture very different from that of conscious thinking." From a normative point of view, it is "pathological," "autoerotic," "schizophrenic" and "sociopathic" (*CW* 5, §37). The violent antagonism between these two ways of knowing—the shadowing of fantasy by the normative intellect—is a part of modern life. But behind this disenchantment of the world is the decisive shift in Western culture that split off Christian from Pagan, spirit from soul.

Pagans were "people of this world" and "people of this time." They were linked to the cosmos[5] through their daimonic images, and lived in what one scholar has called a "rustling universe," an immediate yet imaginative landscape both literal and psychic.[6] This cosmos was not experienced as a uniform expanse, but as a series of dynamic transformational spaces. These dynamic spaces were marked out by shrines, votive signs, temples, grottoes, groves and springs that indicated sites of "close encounter" with the Gods, demons and Heroes (Fox, 41-46). This psychic landscape was the common heritage of the Pagans: all classes, sexes and ages were connected through the experience of its rites, images and oracles.

Epiphany, the manifestation of spirit in and through the world, marked the sacral character of this cosmos. The images and shrines of the Pagan landscape did not so much commemorate the historic event of an epiphany as they re-created the experience. Images and oracles marked the site of the continuing presence of the Gods. They focused the idea of the numinous and facilitated "easy company with the Gods" in dream and vision (Fox, 675). Through these oracular images the Pagans experienced a time when the Gods moved freely among them. This "golden age" was potentially ever-present, humans and Gods "in open company in a generous, burgeoning world" (Fox, 111).

The capacity for epiphany, the ability to experience spirit in the world, is the defining feature of Paganism and of Pagan "fantasy-thinking." Out of this experiential base grew Hermetic magic, the Mystery Cults, theurgy and Neoplatonic gnosis. The oracles, images and verbal formulae developed in this magical tradition were seen as produced by the Gods themselves as "binding spells" through which they might be contacted. A *daimon* or *genius*, an intermittent stream of images, regulated and shaped the personality. An act of mutual creation characterized this world: the magical animation, the en-souling, of an image, shrine, or temple; and especially the incantation of an oracle or spell.

It was just this animating connection between the world and the individual that the Christian Church sought to destroy. For Christians wanted the "obedience" of Pagans (*Romans* 15, 18-19). Apart from the torture of prophets at major shrines (Fox 673-

681), the triumphant Church of the 4th century did not perse-
cute Pagans as such. Rather they destroyed the shrines and images, cut down the groves, despoiled the landscape and prohib-
ited on pain of death the magical and oracular practices that gave
the Gods a voice in the human world. As Eusebius recounted,
they sent an iconoclastic emissary to "every pagan temple's re-
cess and every gloomy cave."

This process, which went on throughout the 4th and 5th centuries, came to be expressed in a myth current in Europe until
the Enlightenment, a myth which continued to express the psychological relations between Pagan imagination and Christian
spirit.[7] Briefly stated, the myth held that upon the advent of
Christ, "the false *Oracles* and *Delusions* [were miraculously]
struken mute, and nothing to be heard at Delphos or Hammon"
(Patrides, 507; quoting Sir Henry Wotton, 1654). Though the
historical process was a bit different, the myth expressed a psychological truth: at the sign of the Cross the *daimones* vanish.

"On the Morning of Christ's Nativity," Milton tells us (stanza
xix):

> The oracles are dumb,
> No voice or hideous hum
>   Runs through the archéd roof in words deceiv-
>   ing.
> Apollo from his shrine
> Can no more divine,
>   With hollow shriek the steep of Delphos leav-
>   ing.
> No nightly trance or breathéd spell,
> Inspires the pale-eyed priest from the prophetic
>   cell.

"A voice of weeping and great lament" is heard, rising from
mountains, shores, "haunted springs," "consecrated earth," "holy
hearth," altars, tombs and groves as the nymphs, Lares, Lemures,
Gods and Goddesses "forsake their temples dim." The "flocking

shadows pale/ troop to the infernal jail/ each fettered ghost slips to his several grave." No other spirit, God, nymph or daimon "longer dare abide" when "Our Babe" shows his "Godhead true."

The Pagan lightbringer Lucifer's lament,[8] as he is cast in the role of adversary of an implacable God, strikes the modern reader in a very different way from what Milton intended:

> Me miserable! which way shall I fly
> Infinite wrath and infinite despair?
> Which way I fly is Hell; myself am Hell
> And in the lowest deep a lower deep
> Still threatening to devour me opens wide...
> (Paradise Lost, iv, 73-77)

This "light of nature,"[9] wayfinder and psychopomp, is the God in our disease.

Lights and Shadows: Like(ness) cures Like

Whatever the social or philosophical dimensions[10] of the splitting-off of "Christian" from "Pagan," its psychological importance cannot be overstated. The point at which the Holy Spirit demonized the Pagan "spirits" was a decisive event for world culture. The shadow that fell on the Gods, the flesh, and the cosmos fell on all races and cultures in the spread of European science and power, demonizing and repressing them in the same way Pagan Mediterranean culture was demonized and repressed.

Phenomenologically, this splitting produces two opposed ways of relating (*imago*) to that "ocean of images and figures" which "alone constitutes immediate experience" (*CW* 8, § 674, 680). The *spiritual imago* is converted to the Holy Spirit, while the *psychic imago* is split off and *projected* as the shadow; it *demonizes* whatever it touches.

Shadow *occults*, it "conceals and causes to disappear from view" through a process of repression, creating a screen of moral opacity between the ego and an Other. Yet this web of hot, dark inferiority—the sordid behavior described in Paul's version of the Pagans, for example (*Romans* 1, 24-32)—*saves* as well as demonizes. Shadow *carries* what is most feared by the ego as a threat to its self-image.

Projection, whereby these negative subjective contents are then expelled onto an object (*CW* 6, §783), has an even more profound effect on the subject. Through this expulsion, there begins an ever-increasing manic spiral of incompletion, sterility and fear that is, in its turn, explained as "the malevolence of the environment and, by means of this vicious circle, the isolation [of the subject] is intensified" (*CW* 9ii, §17). The only way to cut into this soulless round is a confrontation with the "unknown face" of the shadow. For the occulted psyche, by its very nature, has the capacity to re-join the split in our experience if it is allowed *by the individual* to return from its exile in the unconscious.[11]

When we move through shadow to image rather than through reason to fact we are *making soul*, creating the opportunity, opening the *kairos* through which the world is re-imagined. This is the "psychic connection" at the heart of the Pagan cosmos, the "ritual landscape" with its points of close encounter. It is also the central concern of all divinatory systems, of the act of divination itself: to move through the shadow of the literal situation, towards a psycho-active force which is demanding access to consciousness.

"Like cures like" is a fundamental principle of traditional medicine: the cure is (like) the disease. But likenesses[12] are *not* sames. As in homeopathic medicine, the "cure" is the drug which causes the symptom, highly diluted and imaginally empowered. It is the symptom transformed into a demon. This transformation itself has a deep significance. When we touch on this dark gap, "the realm of subtle bodies comes to life

again...the physical and the psychic are once more blended"
(*CW* 12, §394).

The Light of Nature and Liminal Space

The insight into psychic functioning developed in ancient medicine, myth and divination is also expressed in modern archetypal psychology. This perspective forces us to recognize a very old psychic fact:

> ...within the affliction is a complex, within the complex is an archetype, which in turn refers to a God. Afflictions point to Gods: Gods reach us through afflictions...[they] *force themselves symptomatically into awareness.*
> (Hillman, *Re-visioning Psychology*, 104-5)

Thus the divinatory question: "To what God do I owe my affliction? What imaginal act, what imagining must I perform in order to see-through this opaque situation? How can I come into conscious relation with the God?"

But the heart of the divinatory practice which reveals the Pagan cosmos is not the individual God *per se*. "What the Gods notoriously want is remembrance of them, not choice among them, so that every conflict—and the very question Who?—by asking which among many, indicates them all" (Hillman, *Re-visioning Psychology*, 139).

Or, as Bouché-Leclercq's classic study of Greco-Roman divinatory systems puts it:

> The religious conceptions of Greece and Rome enclosed a profoundly mystical element implanted in all its customs...the belief in a permanent revelation proffered by gods to men, a sort of spontaneous intellectual aid...thanks to which societies and individuals could regulate their acts. The gods, from this point of view, are no longer exigent creditors or indifferent abstractions but benevolent counselors whose voice signalled, at the

opportune moment, the price of the present occasion, the se-
crets of the past or the traps of the future. The Greeks called
mantike and the Latins *divinatio* this divine light which added
itself, like a new faculty, to human comprehension.[13]

Studies of "live" divinatory systems in tribal cultures[14] tell us
that divination is not a random act by an aberrant individual,
charlatan or power-seeker, nor is it a device used to maintain a
ruling ideology. Rather, it is a process deriving from a discipline
and a body of knowledge which consistently yields information
about questions, problems and choices for which rational
knowledge is insufficient. Some type of "device" involving
chance or accident provides the "gap" through which the spirit
expresses itself. The final diagnosis and plan of action emerge
from an interpretive interaction.

The divinatory process is not an ideology founded on religious
belief but a dynamic way of knowing. These systems combine
"logical-analytical" and "intuitive-synthetic" modes of thinking
that in European thought are rigidly separated. They shift deci-
sion-making into a liminal realm by simultaneously operating in
opposing cognitive modes (Peek, *Divination Systems*, 2-3). In
tribal cultures, these systems are often sponsored by a "rival
creator," an animal trickster figure such as Gray Fox or Monkey
whose potent enigmas offer an alternative to more public, legal-
istic truth (Shaw, *Divination Systems*, 140-141). Through their
use a liminal space opens where violent emotional states, dreams,
diseases—encounters with the force of the Gods—are turned
into individual psychic awareness. The goal of divination underlies the goal of philosophy: a purification of the soul which saves
the reality of the Gods and enables the inquirer to understand
the intelligence that is given by them to humans (Lain Entralgo,
128).

In English, the words "oracle" and "divination" describe this
process. *Oracle* refers to the shrine consecrated to a God, the
space set off for contact, as well as to the priest, medium or

transmitter and to the words or counsel given: the enigma or dark saying that links the God and the inquirer. "Oracle" emphasizes a magical, god-producing quality in the words that ordinarily form our human community.

Divination refers to the act of foretelling the movement of events or revealing hidden forces. In modern English the term has strong overtones of superstition and charlatanism. Yet, as in Latin, divination contains the "divine" and gives it a vehicle.

There is a third word we must add to these to understand divination systems: to *symbolize*, thought of as a transitive verb. Originally given to the halves of a tablet that was broken when two men became "guest-friends," the Greek word *symballon* was also used for the engraved shells carried by initiates of Mystery cults as signs of a mutual encounter with the numinous. It came to include linking tokens of all kinds: military passwords, corporate insigniae, wedding bands, the ring a guest gave at a banquet or symposium as promise of payment, a permit given to aliens allowing them to reside in the city.

To empower something as a symbol, to "symbolize" it, is a fundamental act of the human soul. It creates a liminal space through which one is put in contact with the "Others," with what is behind immediate sensible reality. Divinatory processes create, maintain, and evolve symbols. An interesting Biblical use of the term is *Luke* 2.19. After the shepherds told Mary of the signs of the Saviour given to them by angels, she "preserved these sayings (*rhêma*), symbolizing them (*symballô*) in her heart."

Symbolizing *values*. It withdraws a word or phrase from common currency and allows it to "flower" in the heart. In the empowering of symbols and in the access to liminal space that it provides, a divinatory system involves the user with a "spirit" not cut off from psyche, a "light of nature" previous to the splitting of psyche and spirit which produced the demonization of our world.

Ting: the Other's Vessel

The *Yi Ching* or *Chou Yi*[15] is perhaps the oldest and most complex divinatory system that survives. It is one of the few oracles outside of tribal cultures which still contains a "living spirit" (*CW* 15, §78). It represents a process or way of knowing that is antithetical to modern positivism. Its oldest texts go back to a time when the roots of a divinatory science were first emerging from shamanism.[16]

Jung saw the divinatory use of the *Yi Ching* and its rhetoric of archetypes as a background to the emergence of Western psychology (*CW* 18, §139). This perception was at the heart of his elaboration of "synchronicity" as an irrational connecting factor compensating the one-sidedness of rational causality.[17] For him, the *Yi Ching* was the basis of an Eastern science with psychological premises radically different from Western rationalism (*CW* 15, §80). Its language was the language of dreams, myths and alchemical symbols.

Jung's concern with Hellenistic Mystery Cults and the *daimones*, his own "initiation" during the long "fallow period" of his fantasies, his involvement with alchemical symbolism—all form part of a life-long attempt to darken the Christ-figure of Western culture, to enter its shadow.[18] Thus he would, he felt, "dream the myth onward"[19] through its Pagan shadow and the mystery of psyche, daimon and cosmos.

The sense of history Jung entertains here links the divinatory power of the *Yi Ching* and the "spirit of tao" he found in Chinese philosophy with the West's own "pre-scientific psychology." The *Yi Ching* enters our imagination through the *shadow side* of Western tradition: pre-Socratic philosophers, Gnostics, alchemists, theurgic magicians, Neoplatonists, astrologers, diviners and mediums, Paracelsus, Agrippa—all part of an occulted world-view which "underlies all the magical and mantic procedures that have played an important part in man's life since the remotest times" (*CW* 8, §939-40). The "living spirit of the East" in the *Yi Ching* (*CW* 15, §78) brings back to life a way of thought outlawed in the West since Late Antiquity: something "almost taboo, outside the scope of our judgments," (*CW* 15 §80), lingering in the "twilight" of Christian culture (*CW* 15 §85), in "our own darkness" (*CW 15*, §88), "something in *us* that is in need of further development" (*CW* 15 §86). As an occult search for individual "meaning" (Richard Wilhelm's translation [*der Sinn*] of the Chinese term *tao*) this "could be a dangerous infection, but it might also be a remedy" for the "arrogance and tension of the European will" (*CW* 15, § 90).

The divinatory use of the *Yi Ching* points to the shadow because its "living spirit" *is* the shadow of Christianity. It *recreates* this way of knowing, dimming the bright light of conscious will, directing energy to the "complexes" or demons.

Thus Jung saw the oracle technique of the *Yi Ching* as "a method of exploring the unconscious" (*CW* 11, §966). The projection of subjective contents into the oracle's symbols was an integral part of the procedure, for the masks and magic spells of this "dreamlike" system *translate* the inquirer's concerns into the language of the liminal. This creates a gap, a "dragon hole" where the intervention of unconscious contents can change the inquirer's universe of thought. In this dynamic interchange between conscious and unconscious both are moved. The energetic relation between them is adjusted, and *shen ming*, "bright spirit" or "the light of the Gods" emerges. It is the experience of this way of knowing, more than any specific counsel, that is the goal of the process.

Hexagram 50, TING, *The Vessel/Holding*, is the image of an elaborately crafted and decorated cast bronze vessel used to cook food offered to humans, ancestral spirits and the Gods. It links these worlds through ritual procedures involving "symbolizing" or creating symbols. For Jung (*CW* 11, 982), the *Yi Ching* itself was a *Ting*:

...a vessel in which sacrificial offerings are brought to the gods... a cult object serving to provide spiritual nourishment for the unconscious elements or forces...to give these forces the attention they need in order to play their part in the life of the individual.

The Name of the Book

The central concern of the *Yi Ching* links it to those moments in life when one faces the encounter with an "alien" through a personal crisis or conflict. This is expressed by the key term *yi*, sometimes translated as "change" or "changes." The book derives its oracular function from this term. The second term, *ching*, is an honorific for classical or canonical books. The *Yi Ching* is the classic, constant, channel or loom of *yi*.

Yi in the human world can only be understood in terms of three other key themes: *tao*, *te*, and *chün tzu*. *Tao*, literally "way," is a central term in most Eastern thought. It refers to the "way" in which everything happens and the way on which everything happens. *Te*, often translated as "power" or "virtue," refers to the process of manifesting *tao* in individual life and action. It suggests a straightening of the inner essence which permits a being to become what it is intrinsically meant to be. The *chün tzu* is the ideal user of the book. A *chün tzu*, literally "chief son," is someone who strives to conform to his or her inherent destiny as a specific manifestation of *tao*. One is a *chün tzu* insofar as one turns to the oracle in order to organize one's life according to *tao* and the soul's images rather than wilful intentions.

The first meaning of the term *yi* emphasizes mobility, openness and fluidity. It suggests the ability to change direction quickly and radically, a flexible many-sidedness that uses a variety of talents. The most adequate English translation of this is "versatility," the ability to remain available to the unforeseen demands of time, fate and *tao*. This term interweaves the *yi* of the cosmos, the *yi* of the book, and the *yi* of one who uses it to manifest *tao*.

Another context for *yi* highlights a connection with breakdown and flux. This is a discussion between King Wen and a disaffected Shang prince. King Wen was spiritual father of the Chou Dynasty (c. 1000 - 480 BCE), who spent several years in the prisons of the preceeding Shang Dynasty (c. 1520 - 1030 BCE).

> [King Wen] said: What the king scrutinizes is the year, the dignitaries and noblemen the months, the many lower officials the days. When in years, months, days, the season has no *yi*, the many cereals ripen, the administration is enlightened, talented men of the people are distinguished, the house is peaceful and at ease. When in days, months, years, the season has *yi*, the many cereals do not ripen, the administration is dark and unenlightened, talented men of the people are in petty positions, the house is not at peace.[20]

Yi is not the orderly change of the seasons or the transformation of one thing into another. It originates in and is a way of dealing with "trouble." It articulates the possible responses to fate, necessity, calamity: those demons which "cross" your path.

The actual name of the book is *Chou Yi*, i.e. the *yi* or versatility-book of the Chou Dynasty. The term *chou*, however, can be imagined in another way, for it keeps its intrinsic meaning even when used as a proper name. Intrinsically, *chou* means "universal, to encompass everything." Thus the concern and the aim of the book, its ethical core, might best be translated as *Encompassing Versatility*. It is an oracular text that seeks to image the individual in terms of the all-encompassing and ever-changing movement of *tao* and the *chün tzu's* adaptation to it through *yi*, versatility.

The *Classic of Yi* was the basis of much of traditional Chinese civilization. Its images provided a semiotic reservoir for popular culture, religious belief and the most elaborate philosophical and numerological speculations. Underlying all this, however, was the experience that, when stimulated by consultation, the oracle is "continuous with the causal conditions in the all-under-heaven," describing the seeds of events in the world and in the human heart. Thus it is a "mysterious and potent duplicate of that which is numinous."[21] In this context, the *Yi Ching's* "magic spells" are healing images, links to regenerating forces in the *anima mundi*, the soul of the world. Work with these "magic spells" is also a healing of the images themselves, re-constituting the occulted world of psyche and its demons.

Spirits and Symbols: The God in the Disease

The *Yi Ching* consists of a set of oracular texts, organized and displayed through a system of 64 six-line figures or *kua*, usually translated as *hexagrams*: all the possible combinations of six whole (——) and/or opened (— —) lines. It is these lines which are produced by the chance or random consultative process. Together, the texts and figures provide a rhetoric of the archetypes, a vocabulary of the possible modes of being and change. Through the consultation process what the normative mind sees as chance or accident is empowered as a symbolic occurance, a linking of the literal and the imaginal. Use of this system represents religion at its most fundamental level: attention to the psychic images that trigger, co-ordinate and transform what we call "instinct" (*CW* 14, §602-3).

Two terms from the *Hsi tz'u chuan*,[22] a treatise appended to the hexagram texts in the Han Dynasty (206 BCE - 220 CE), expand on this process. These terms and the oral interpretive tradition that lies behind them come from the Warring States Period (c. 400 - 220 BCE),[23] a period of political conflict in China that also gave rise to the fundamental Taoist and Confucian texts. It was during this period that a more individual use of the yarrow-stalk oracle began.

According to this commentary, the function of the *Yi* is to provide symbols (*hsiang*; B3.1). It has in it the course traced by the on-going process (*tao*) of heaven, earth and humans (B10.2-4; Peterson, 89) and it makes numinous (*shen*) that conduct which is imaginatively potent (A9.18; Peterson, 104-5). In itself still and unmoving (A10.15), when stimulated by consultation it produces an echo which reaches the depths and grasps the seeds (A10.18), comprehending the causes in the realm of all-under-heaven (A10.16; Peterson, 106). The shamans and sages who created its symbols drummed and danced in order to bring out the spirits or *shen* (A12.13; Peterson, 107). In the same way these symbols speak to the unconscious mind of the inquirer, evoking an imaginative process which "completes the ceaseless activity of heaven" (Schultz, 186).

The *chün tzu*, the ideal user of the book, immerses himself in the *Yi* and its symbols, observing the figures obtained through divination and taking joy in their words. By turning and rolling these words in his heart (A2.10-11), the *chün tzu* allows them to symbolize (*hsiang*) the situation, bringing out and fulfilling the spirits or *shen* (A12.13; Schultz, 186).

Hsiang, "symbolize", empowers an image as archetypal and perceives in it the power to connect the visible and the invisible. To do this is called *shen*, which refers to: spirit, spirits, what is numinous or spiritually potent. The oracle was symbolized or empowered (*hsiang*) to further *shen* and to create *shen ming*, bright spirit or the light of the Gods.

Like the shamans and sage-kings of old, this commentary says, the one who uses the *Yi's* symbolizing power re-creates the numinous world, acquiring helping-spirit, or *shen* (A9.19; Peterson, 105/107). The *Yi* is not itself a demon. It is a maker of demons, an imaginative discipline that allows its users to experience a demon within themselves as an in-forming and regulating force. The oracle exists as a dynamic field of meaning between the user and his or her demon. This field is continually evolving, and is re-created in each consultation through the archetypal mystery

of its symbols. Opening this symbolic reality can have a syn-
chronous effect on both the individual and the world. It can be
an epiphanic experience of that golden age when the Gods and
humans met. In the irrational and subversive encounter with the
demons of divination, we experience ourselves once again en-
souled, as spirits in an imagined world.

NOTES

1. John Milton, *Paradise Lost*, iv, 75; *Collected Works*, ed. Helen Darbishire, 2
vol. (Oxford: Oxford University Press, 1952-5). All references are to this
edition.
2. "Le Poète se fait *voyant* par un long, immense et raisonné *dérèglement* de
tout les sens. Toutes les formes d'amour, de souffrance, de folie; il cherche lui-
même, il épuise en lui tous les poisons...it devient entre tous le grand malade,
le grand criminel, le grand maudit—et le suprême Savant—car il arrive à l' *in-
connu!*" Letter to Paul Demeny (15 May 1871): Arthur Rimbaud, *Oeuvres*, ed.
S. Bernard and A. Guyax (Paris: Bordas, Classiques Garnier, 1991), p. 348.
3. *CW* 9i, §40; references to Jung's *Collected Works* (*CW*) are to Bollingen Series XX, vol. 1-20, tr. R. F. C. Hull (Princeton: Princeton University Press,
1957-79).
4. This is elaborated in particular in Paul's *Epistle to the Romans*, which
formed the basis of later Christian theory culminating in Augustine's *De Civi-
tate Dei*.
5. The Greek term *kosmos* links "order" with "ornament" and "intelligence."
The visible world (*kosmos aisthêtôs*), which is the "visible God" (*horatos theos*), is
in constant mimetic interaction with the "intelligible world" (*kosmos noêtos*).
Image, intelligence and spirit are not in rivalry in "*kosmos*." Jung perceived
that this "sacred cosmos" was the equivalent of the psyche itself. See Jean
Pépin, "Cosmic Piety," in *Classical Mediterranean Spirituality*, vol. 15 of *World
Spirituality* (New York: Crossroads, 1986), pp. 408-435.
6. Peter Brown, *Body and Society* (New York: Columbia University Press,
1988), p. 27. See also R. L. Fox, *Pagans and Christians* (New York: Alfred
Knopf, 1987), pp. 608-662; A. H. Armstrong. "Itineraries in Late Antiquity,"
Eranos 56-1987, pp. 105-132, and "The Ancient and Continuing Pieties," *Classi-
cal Mediterranean Spirituality*, vol. 15 of *World Spirituality* (New York: Cross-
roads, 1986); Peter Brown, *The World of Late Antiquity* (London: Thames and
Hudson, 1971); E.R. Dodds, *Pagan and Christian in an Age of Anxiety*
(Cambridge, 1956); A. J. Festugière, *Personal Religion among the Greeks*
(Berkeley: University of California Press, 1954).

7. See C.A. Patrides, "The Cessation of the Oracles: the History of a Legend," *PMLA* 60/4, 1963, pp. 500-507; and James Hillman, *Pan and the Nightmare* (New York: Spring Publications, 1972), particularly p. 1i. On the myth that Christ forever closed the doors to the Underworld, see F. Huidekoper, *The Belief of the First Three Centuries Concerning Christ's Mission to the Underworld* (New York: James Miller, 1876); and James Hillman, *The Dream and the Underworld* (New York: Harper and Row, 1979), Chapter 4 on "Barriers."

8. Lucifer (literally "light-bearer") became in Christian myth a rebel archangel whose fall from heaven was referred to in *Isaiah* 14.12: "How thou art fallen, oh day-star, son of the morning." This Old Testament passage, part of a polemic against the King of Babylon, was interpreted to mean that the chief of the angels who "kept not their estate" was named Lucifer before he fell, thereafter Satan, the Adversary. This Lucifer was identified with *Phosphoros* and the *Phosphoroi*, a term in Pagan cults which referred both to the "morning and evening star" and to a particular shining or revealing quality associated with the Gods—a quality that was, in fact, prior to the Olympian cults. Thus Hestia's hearthfire, Hermes' wayfinding, Artemis' knowledge of the wilds, Hekate's dark wisdom, Selene's shining, Persephone's underworld knowing, Pan's spontaneity and Aphrodite's beauty were all a quality of "*phosphoros*." See W.H. Roscher, *Lexikon der Griechischen und Römischen Mythologie* (Leipzig, 1902-1909: rpt. Hildesheim: Georg Olms Verlag, 1978), III, p. 2, entry "*phosphoroi/ Phosphoros*." It was this identification that allowed Christian apologists to maintain with Augustine that "*Omnes dii gentium daemonia* / all the gods of the pagans are demons," (*Enn. Psal.*, PS 96. PL xxxvi, 1231-32) and that these demons are the devil. Thus they turned Lucifer into Satan, the Adversary of J*HW*H, the Old Testament God. Another often used passage was *Genesis* 6 in which the "sons of God" who were set over men "fell" through copulation with the "daughters of men," thus producing a race of demons. These too were identified with the Pagan Gods (Justin, 2 *Apol.* 128: see *Encyclopedia of Religion and Ethics*, ed. James Hastings, 12 vol. [Edinburgh: T & T Clark, 1908-21], entry "demons and spirits: Christian.") All of these demons were seen to occupy themselves particularly with the divination and magic which was their "light" (Augustine, c. *Academ.*, i.19.20).

9. In alchemical terms, *lumen naturae* is the "light of nature" as opposed to the *numen* of spiritual revelation. It is a *sol invisibilis* given to the individual, accessible through and identical with the "subtle" or "astral" body (*ôchema pneuma*). It offers each individual "sufficient predestined light that he err not" (*CW* 8, §390; quoting Paracelsus). Phenomenologically, *lumen naturae* is experienced as *scintillae* or sparks of the world soul scattered throughout the dark sea of night, germinal luminosities which are the seedbed of worlds to come (*mundi futuri seminarium; CW* 8, §388). This natural force, also described as an underworld fire, or *ignis mercurialis*, is synonymous with the Pagan *cosmos* and *aion* (*CW* 13, §256).

10. Jung theorized about the "necessity" of Christianity on two not necessarily connected levels. First, he speculated the "flight from the world" had been dialectically necessary to build up a "type of thinking independent of external factors," the "sovereignty of the idea," which then entered into a new relation with Nature (*CW* 5, §113). Thus there existed for Jung a "golden age:" the "fantastic mythological world of the [High] Middle Ages" (*CW* 18, §1363) when the *numen* of spiritual revelation co-existed with the *lumen* of revived Pagan spirit. His fascination and identification with Paracelsus (1493-1541), a Swiss alchemical philosopher of "prescient ideas" who could still hold the *numen* and *lumen* together, is a reflection of this (*CW* 8, §388-393; *CW* 13, §148, 197-200). On the Antique World in the Middle Ages see Jean Seznec, *The Survival of the Pagan Gods*, tr. B. Sessions (New York: Pantheon, Bollingen Series XXXVIII, 1953); and Valerie Flint, *The Rise of Magic in Early Medieval Europe* (Princeton: Princeton University Press, 1991).

Secondly, Christianity was "a frantic and desperate attempt to create—out of no matter how doubtful material—a spiritual monarch, a *pantocrator*, in opposition to the concretized divinity of Rome" (*CW* 18, §1568). It arose in opposition to the "whirlwinds of brutality and unchained libido that roared through the streets of Imperial Rome" (*CW* 5, § 104) and answered the "strange melancholy and longing for deliverance" of a society where three-fifths of the population were slaves (*CW* 10, §249-250). This view was intensified by Jung's identification of the rise of the dictators in Europe with both the old German God of "storm and frenzy," Wotan, (*CW* 10, "Wotan," § 371-399) and with a return to the "brutality" of Rome (*CW* 5, §341). Jung's deeper sense of the Pagan as *psyche* was often lost in this panic. See James Hillman, "Dionysos in Jung's Writing," *Spring* 1972, pp. 191-205.

11. James Hillman, "Senex and Puer," in *Puer Papers* (Dallas: Spring Publications, 1989), p. 14. On "soul-making," creating an imaginative cosmos, see James Hillman, *Re-visioning Psychology* (New York: Harper and Row, 1975), particularly ix-xvii and Chapter 4.

12. The Greek word is *homoioma*. It suggests: to make a likeness, to experience being "like" but not identical with, to become like. This is, according to Paul (*Romans* 1, 18-23), the great sin of the Pagans. They hold the Spirit captive (*crateô*) in the cheating lies (*pseudo*) which are their images (*eikon*). Thus they exchange the glory of the Lord for likeness or likening (*homoioma*). The "psychic" Pagans worship and serve (*esebathêsan kai elateusan*: technical terms of cult) the creatures, abandoning the creator.

Through this use of the term *homoioma*, the spirit in Paul is collapsing a "way of knowing." *Homoios* is the basis of psychological knowledge, *magia* and science: that "like is known by like or likeness." The knower knows the known through a likening element between them, and in this knowing the subject becomes "like" though not identical with that which is known. It is a principle of likening to spirit (*homoiôsis theô*) for which images are necessary.

They constitute the *relatedness* (*sympatheia*) of things. This "likening" ensouls ritual acts, divinatory processes, and Mystery Cults. The imaginative process evoked in *homoioma* "expresses a mystery that reaches down into the history of the human mind...far beyond the beginnings of Christianity...Man expresses his most fundamental and most important psychological conditions in this ritual, this magic...the cult performance of basic psychological facts" (*CW* 18, §616-617).

13. A. Bouché-Leclercq, *Histoire de la divination dans l'antiquité*, 4 vol. (Paris, 1879; rpt. Aalen: Scientia Verlag, 1978), vol. 1, pp. 1-6, my translation. See also H. W. Parke, *Greek Oracles* (London, 1967) and R. Flacelière, *Devins et oracles grecs* (Paris, 1961).

14. *African Divination Systems: Ways of Knowing*, ed. Phillip M. Peek (Bloomington, Indiana: Indiana University Press, 1991). I cite in the following discussion: Phillip Peek, "The Study of Divination, Present and Past," pp. 1-22 and "African Divination Systems: Non-Normal Modes of Cognition," pp. 193-212; Roslind Shaw, "Splitting Truths from Darkness: Epistomological Aspects of Temne Divination," pp. 137-152; and James W. Fernandez, "Afterword," pp. 213-222. The classic study of an African tribal divination system is William Bascomb, *Ifa Divination: Communication between Gods and Men in West Africa* (Bloomington, Indiana: Indiana University Press, 1969; rpt. 1991). See also Pedro Lain Entralgo, *The Therapy of the Word in Classical Antiquity*, eds. and trs. L. J. Rather and John M. Sharp (New Haven: Yale University Press, 1970), p. xviii. Relevant in another sense is James Hillman's discussion of *peitho* (persuasive words) and *ananké* (necessity) in "On the Necessity of Abnormal Psychology: Ananke and Athene," *Facing the Gods* (Dallas: Spring Publications, 1980), particularly pp. 18-21. Plato maintained that the cosmos comes into being when Nous, the intuitive mind, persuades (*peitho*) Ananke, i.e. offers her the "persuasive words" (*Tim.* 47e-48a) of spell, oracle or philosophy.

15. The Chinese text used is *Harvard-Yenching Institute Sinological Index Series, Supplement 10: A Concordance to the Yi Ching* (rpt. Taipei: Chinese Materials and Research Aids Service Center, Inc., 1966). This reproduces, with a Concordance, the last of the "classic" editions of the text, the *Chou-i-chê-chung* or Palace Edition of 1715. English translation and explanatory materials come from *Chou Yi: The Oracle of Encompassing Versatility*, 3 vol., *Eranos 58-1989, 59-1990* and *60-1991*. Apart from a small group of perennially contested "loan-words," the fundamental text and appendices have remained stable since the late Han Dynasty (200 BCE - 200 CE). Changes in interpretation of these mysterious texts have marked significant cultural shifts in Chinese history. The current interpretive strategy is based on "*yi gu*" or "scepticism towards antiquity" and it characterized by what an American practitioner has called a "ruthless literal-mindedness" (Kunst, viii). For an overview of the attitude and the scholarship see Richard Kunst, *The Original Yijing: A Text, Phonetic Tran-*

scription, Translation and Indexes (Ann Arbor, Michigan: University Microfilms International, 1985) which includes an extensive bibliography.

16. On the history of divinatory methods in China, see Léon Vandermeersch, "De la tortue à l'achillée" in *Divination et rationalité* (Paris: Editions du Seuil, 1974) pp. 29-51, and "The Origin of Milfoil Divination and the Primitive Form of the *I Ching*," paper presented at the Workshop on Divination and Portent Interpretation in Ancient China, University of California, Berkeley, June 20-July 1, 1983, rpt. (French) *Hexagrammes* 4/1989, pp. 5-24; and Michael Loewe, "China," in *Oracles and Divination* (Boulder, Colorado: Shambhala, 1981), pp. 38-62.

17. See *Analytical Psychology: Notes of the Seminar Given in 1925 by C.G. Jung*, ed. William McGuire (Princeton: Princeton University Press, Bollingen Series XCIX, 1989), pp. 22-97.

18. See James Hillman, *The Dream and the Underworld*, pp. 89-90. In an early letter to Freud, Jung described his work as an attempt to "…transform Christ back into the soothsaying god of the vine which he was, and in this way absorb those ecstatic instinctual forces of Christianity for the one purpose of making the cult and the myth what they once were—a drunken feast of joy where man regained the ethos and holiness of an animal. That was the beauty and purpose of classical religion, which from God knows what temporary biological needs has turned into a Misery Institute. Yet what infinite rapture and wantonness lies dormant in our religion, waiting to be led back to their true destination! …only this…development can serve the vital forces of religion." *The Freud-Jung Letters*, ed. William McGuire (Princeton: Princeton University Press, 1974), p. 294. See also *CW* 6, §78-93, where an older and more sober Jung struggles with the inherent tendency of Christianity to "paralyze" fantasy and the "specific activity of the psyche."

19. The phrase is from *CW* 9ii, §271: "Even the best attempts at explanation [of the archetype] are only more or less successful translations into another metaphorical language…The most we can do is to *dream the myth onwards* and give it a modern dress." Marie-Louise von Franz summarizes Jung's commitment to "dreaming-on" the Christian archetype in her introduction to *The Zofingia Lectures* (*CW*, Supplementary Volume A), pp. xxiv-xxv.

20. Bernard Karlgren, *The Book of Documents* (texts and translation), reprinted from *Bulletin* XXII/1950 (Stockholm: Museum of Far Eastern Antiquities, 1950), p. 33. Traditionally the *Yi* was created in this "declining era" that marked the end of the Shang and the beginning of the "bountiful potency of the Chou" (*Hsi ts'u*, B2.1, B11.1). Identification with the early Chou rulers was, in later culture, a way of asserting the correctness of one's stance in an otherwise decadent age. See Herrlee G. Creel, *The Birth of China*, (New York: Ungar, 1937) and *The Origins of Statecraft in China*, vol. I (Chicago: University of Chicago Press, 1980); and Hellmut Wilhelm, "Sacrifice in the *I Ching*," *Spring* 1972, rpt. *Heaven, Earth and Man in the Book of Changes* (Seattle: University of

Washington Press, 1977). Many of the songs of the *Shih Ching* or *Book of Songs* (c. 800 BCE) deal with this founding myth.

21. Willard J. Peterson, "Some Connective Concepts in China," *Eranos 57-1988*, pp. 228, 230.

22. The *Hsi tz'u chuan* (*Commentary on the Attached Verbalizations*) or *Ta chuan* (*Great Commentary*) makes up two of the Ten Wings added to the *Chou Yi* when it became a classic in the Han Dynasty. Willard Peterson, "Making Connections: 'Commentary on the Attached Verbalizations' of the Book of Change," *Harvard Journal of Asiatic Studies*, 42/1, June 1982, pp. 67-116, is an excellent analysis of its basic premises, offering a brief discussion of the textual history and a new translation of selected passages. I also refer to Larry Schultz, *Lai Chih-te (1526-1604) and the Phenomenology of the Classic of Change* (Ann Arbor, Michigan: University Microfilms, 1982), a study of an important commentator on the *Chou Yi* and the *Hsi tz'u*. The major English translation (badly outdated) is contained in the Wilhelm/Baynes *I Ching or Book of Changes* (Princeton: Princeton University Press, Bollingen Series XIX, various editions); see also Gerald Swanson, *The Great Treatise: Commentary Tradition to the Book of Changes* (Ann Arbor, Michigan: University Microfilms, 1979). The *Hsi tz'u chuan* was "for two thousand years one of the most important statements in Chinese tradition on knowing how the cosmos worked and how humans might relate to that working" (Peterson, p. 67).

23. On the Warring States Period, a time of political chaos which was also the "golden age of Chinese philosophy," see A. C. Graham, *Disputers of the Tao: Philosophical Argument in Ancient China* (La Salle, Illinois: Open Court, 1989).

SPIRIT AND SOUL IN MATHEMATICS

ROBERT EARLY

Modern mathematics has no soul. By this I mean no sensuality, no opacity, no madness, no death. Mathematics is a stern spirituality, even though secular in content. In the widely-quoted words of Bertrand Russell:

> Mathematics, rightly viewed, possesses...supreme beauty—a beauty cold and austere, like that of sculpture, without appeal to any part of our weaker nature, without the gorgeous trappings of painting or music, yet sublimely pure, and capable of a stern perfection such as only the greatest art can show...Remote from human passions, remote even from the pitiful facts of nature, the generations have gradually created an ordered cosmos, where pure thought can dwell as in its natural home, and where one, at least, of our nobler impulses can escape from the dreary exile of the actual world.[1]

Robert Early is an Assistant Professor of Mathematics at Indiana University of Pennsylvania. He has an M.S. in Physics, an M.A. in Mathematics, and an M.A., Ed. in Counseling.

No appeal to any part of our weaker ("pitiful") nature, and proud of it! Cold abstraction up there among the lofty peaks. It was not always this way.

Mathematics had its origins in Egypt and Babylon, in the practical arithmetic of commerce and the astrological rites of priests. It was a mix of the mundane and the sacred, and all empirical (derived from experience). The ancient Greeks then began a cooking of the subject, introducing deductive reasoning, emphasizing the beauty of abstraction. This *sublimatio* extracted the spirit of mathematics from the soul while maintaining a connection between them.

Take Plato, for instance: philosopher, mathematician, educator. In the *Timaeus*, Plato sets forth two opposing principles at work in the universe: *nous* (reason) and *ananke* (necessity, errancy). *Nous* can be understood as the mathematical intelligence that lies behind the structure of the world and the rational approach used by humans seeking to apprehend knowledge. *Ananke* can be understood as the tendency of things in the world to go astray, contrary to law, and the human tendency to wander and commit errors while in the rational pursuit of knowledge. *Ananke* is, in Hillman's words, "...a way soul enters the world, a way the soul gains truths that could not be encountered through reason alone."[2] In the *Timaeus* it is implied that there is something of a balance between *nous* and *ananke*—*nous* is said to persuade *ananke*, but it is clear *nous* alone cannot explain (or rule) the world. This is an affirmation of both spirit and soul.

Furthermore: The Pythagorean school, of which Plato was perhaps the most famous member, is usually remembered for its number mysticism. But it was not a mysticism of the spirit only. Numbers were identified with qualities (male/female, light/dark, etc.), culminating in a cosmology of balanced opposites which paralleled and overlapped with the cosmology based on the four elements (earth, air, fire, and water). It was, in essence, an alchemy based on mathematics in which number properties and arithmetic became a medium for soul expression.[3] The abstraction, the eternality, the *spirituality* of Greek deductive mathematics should be balanced against this somewhat darker background and foundation.

Since those long ago days the *sublimatio* of mathematics has continued, parallel to and probably part of the anti-image and anti-personification fervor of Western culture which Hillman has described.[4] The Pythagorean imagination (and hence the soul of mathematics) has been left far behind (though in physics it seems to have undergone something of a rediscovery, in a rather spiritual form, in Quantum Theory[5]).

From about 415 A.D. (when the Greek mathematician Hypatia was dismembered by the Christians for her "paganism") up to the Renaissance, mathematics came to be regarded as spiritual training—of little value in itself but a good preparation for the study of theology. With the decline of the Church's influence and the ascent of Reason, mathematics took off on its own spiritual flight. God became a Supreme Mathematician, and mathematical abstraction became divine Revelation and Truth. To be a mathematician meant to be on a spiritual quest.[6] Here essentially is where the situation remained until around 1850, when non-Euclidean geometry first came into acceptance. That a consistent geometry could be developed which did not apply to the world was a devastating blow to mathematics as divine Truth. Also troubling to "common sense" was Cantor's theory of infinite sets and the idea that there could be different orders of infinity.

There have been many other developments since 1850 which have served to further separate mathematics from both Christian theology and common sense. They need not be mentioned here. The end result is that mathematics today is divided into two main perspectives, the pure and the applied. Pure mathematics, based on the axiomatic approach, is seen to be empty of meaning and truth. We cannot say truly what anything "means," because meaning depends on terms intentionally left undefined. In the Formalist extreme, we only have a collection of marks on a paper and a set of operations on these marks. There is no content.

Unfortunately for those who would build towering cathedrals of abstract philosophy upon this foundation, contradictions and paradoxes abound. Here, then, is a rational spirituality emptied of content and full of logical holes.

Applied mathematics, on the other hand, is a collection of models each based on particular concrete interpretations of previously undefined terms. A model can yield powerful statements (but not *truths*) about the world and universe (e.g., Einstein's model of space-time based on Riemannian non-Euclidean geometry; chaos theory based on fractal geometry), but we must remember: a model is only a model. The danger of literalism, of taking the model to be the thing itself (ever-present in spiritual teachings), is loss of the depth and soul of the world. Here, then, is a rational spirituality where meaning is compartmentalized, existing only within the confines of particular models. This is nowhere more true than in physics, where different theories hold for different levels of phenomena (the very large and the very small). It is interesting, considering the spiritual style, that physics is guided by the monotheistic vision of a Grand Unified Theory.

* * *

Each day when I enter a classroom to teach I cannot help dragging the legacy of mathematics with me. For most business majors and many others, mathematics is a requirement to be satisfied, of little interest but part of the training necessary for an ascent into careers, money, and prestige. Our technological society sees mathematics more than other subjects as a type of mental training ("it teaches you how to think"), the foundation for the study of "higher" things (which, of course, no longer means theology but rather computer science, accounting, etc.). Most students who appear to really enjoy mathematics (including mathematics majors, of course) usually seem drawn by the clarity and precision and the satisfaction of being able to successfully

solve problems. These often seem to be mainly spiritual pleas-
ures, however, the joy of timeless things appearing neat and tidy.

If there is no (or little—let's not quibble) soul in mathematics
today, is there soul in the mathematics classroom? Yes, but there
could be more. To a very few students mathematics speaks as it
must have to the Pythagoreans—these students seem to sense the
Mystery in mathematics, feel their imaginations and dreams leading them deeper. Most students, though, experience soul in the
form of pathologizing, the flaring-up of symptoms of all kinds,
protests from the heart (and often, head and/or gut). It is not
easy to be precise, think clearly, perform under pressure.

Not to imply that studying mathematics is wrong from a soul
perspective: for many students, especially eighteen-year- olds, the
drawing apart (*separatio*) of spirit and soul can be a deepening
process, an initiation. (One course in particular, calculus, seems
to fulfill for many students the function of an initiatory experience—terror and insecurity before they take it, relief and self-
confidence after they are finished with it.)

I've taken to encouraging my students to share their fantasies
and dreams, to allow soul to speak in a stronger voice. The situation or aspect of my courses which seems to generate the
strongest soul reactions has proved to be the act of trying to
solve problems on homework assignments and, especially, ex-
ams. The psychological process of trying to *see into* a problem
seems to be associated with a great deal of alchemical imagery.
One example, a fantasy:

> I felt as though I was jumping rope on a razor blade, and with
> each jump blood trickled onto the blank paper below me.

Here there is a playfulness (jumping rope) which is also a
wounding, resulting in a *rubedo* (a reddening of the work). I had
the fantasy that the drops of blood might take the form of a solution, because this woman was very good at mathematics and
never turned in blank pages. Perhaps one can see the

"playfulness which is also a wounding" as the beginnings of a mercurial attitude, that vision which by seeing through things transforms them.[7]

One specific way soul shows itself in the mathematics classroom is by projecting its complexities into apparently simple mathematical concepts. I hear it often after a great struggle: "Why was I making this so hard?" Given what to most students is a straightforward problem, a few always turn it into a labyrinth of confusion, darkness, and frustration. It is, in truth, a move toward depth.

Jung relates in *Memories, Dreams and Reflections* that as a young student he experienced "sheer terror" as he struggled in vain to understand algebra. He could not accept even the most basic concepts—their very simplicity seemed whimsical, "a stupid trick to catch peasants with."[8] One of my hardest jobs as a teacher is to help students see the value of time spent wrestling with themselves this way and not to dismiss it as wasted. A mathematics problem can be a good mirror, and one can learn much from mirrors. It is probably true, also, that some people (like Jung) who struggle in vain to understand the most basic mathematical ideas are not simply projecting, but also have the gift of seeing deeper into mathematics than those of us to whom mathematics comes easy.

Another way that soul shows itself in the mathematics classroom is through error. Hillman links error with errancy (*ananke*), the principle of the soul's wandering.[9] This "soul wandering" seems especially evident in the case of so-called "stupid error," caused by "carelessness." Here the spiritual legacy of mathematics asserts itself strongly. The spirit struggles for perfection, but the soul wanders off in another direction (a protest, sometimes), creating diversions, errors, breathing-holes to the underworld. Spirit, when it finds or is shown the errors, may resolve to try harder, "learn from its mistakes." But this all-too-prevalent attitude tries to cheat soul of its due, and soul (as trickster, now) usually makes the last move.

A more imaginative approach might be to allow errors, especially "stupid errors," their voice, so as to legitimate both the soul's wandering tendencies and our own individual backwardness, retardedness, "stupidity." The spiritual style of mathematics need not always be coupled to a spiritual classroom environment. Suppose mathematics teachers could see themselves more as poets instead of spiritual trainers?

Let us allow soul to finish this paper, have the last word. Here is the end of a dream of a freshman in a Probability and Statistics course. It reminds us again that although the study of mathematics is in many ways an ascent, the realm of number goes down deep into soul. Though this shadowy realm can no longer be found in the body of knowledge we consider to be "mathematics," it lurks just below the surface in the mathematics classroom and in those who study mathematics.

> ...The hill is so big. I must climb it, though. There is no other way out. As I climb, there they are again. The numbers! Numbers, Numbers, Numbers! Why can't I escape them? I use the fours to step up, the eights to hold onto. Knowing, that the hill of numbers could collapse at any time. I am so afraid. I manage to continue climbing, but before I reach the top of the hill of numbers, I am awake.
>
> This dream disturbs me, because I feel that if only I could reach the top, I could have the answers. However, the numbers will not permit me to. They just continue haunting me by teasing me in my dreams.

NOTES

1. Bertand Russell, *Mysticism and Logic* (New York: Doubleday, 1957) pp. 57-58.

2. James Hillman, *Re-Visioning Psychology* (New York: Harper & Row, 1975) pp. 159-160.

3. For a discussion of Jabirian alchemy and Pythagorean number theory, see C.A. Wilson, "Jabirian Numbers, Pythagorean Numbers and Plato's *Timeaus*" *Ambix* 35.1 (1988). For an analysis of the metaphorical connections between Pythagorean number theory, music and cosmology, see E. McClain, *The Pythagorean Plato: Prelude to the Song Itself* (Stony Brook, N.Y.: Nicolas Hays, 1978).

4. See, for instance, James Hillman, "Peaks and Vales," *Puer Papers* (Dallas: Spring, 1979) and Hillman, *Re-Visioning Psychology*.

5. Marie-Louise von Franz, *Number and Time* (Evanston: Northwestern University Press, 1974) pp. 46-50.

6. M. Kline, *Mathematics in Western Culture* (New York: Oxford University Press, 1953), p. 108.

7. Student fantasies and dreams show a wide variety of alchemical imagery (*calcinatio, solutio, mortificatio...*). For examples and discussion see R. Early, "The Alchemy of Mathematical Experience: A Psychoanalysis of Student Writings," *For the Learning of Mathematics* 12.1 (1992).

8. C. G. Jung, *Memories, Dreams, Reflections* (New York: Vantage, 1965), pp. 27-28.

9. Hillman, *Re-Visioning Psychology*, p. 159.

READING JUNG BACKWARDS?

THE CORRESPONDENCE BETWEEN MICHAEL FORDHAM AND RICHARD HULL CONCERNING "THE TYPE PROBLEM IN POETRY" IN JUNG'S *PSYCHOLOGICAL TYPES*

SONU SHAMDASANI

The editing and translation into English of the *Collected Works* of Jung was the largest scale scholarly project ever undertaken in the world of Analytical Psychology, yet it has received scant attention to date. It is little appreciated that in the course of this endeavour, the editors and translators had to grapple with complex textual and historical matters concerning the reading of Jung's work that have by no means been resolved to this day.

One reason for this occlusion is that the bulk of the discussions of these issues took place in the correspondence between the editors and translators, which has not been published. The most regrettable consequence of this has been the virtual disappearance of Richard Hull. Hull's correspondence, some of which is publicly available in the Bollingen Archive in the Library of Congress, shows him to have been a witty, acerbic and astute commentator on Jung. It has been a great loss that his capability

Sonu Shamdasani is editor of Théodore Flournoy's *From India to the Planet Mars* (Princeton University Press) and *Speculations after Freud: Psychoanalysis, Philosophy, Culture* (Routledge).

as a commentator, rather than simply as a translator, has not been more widely known. In his autobiography, Michael Fordham recalls Hull as follows: "...he had a beautiful mind and his translations were a pleasure to read even though they are sometimes criticised for 'improving' too much on the original Jung!"[1]

The publication of a segment of the editorial correspondence serves to further document the history of the editing of the *Collected Works*.[2] In addition, the editorial correspondence forms a convenient starting point for a closer consideration of Jung's texts, as they raise issues that are still of concern. For they pose the question not only of the interpretation of Jung's text, but how one is to read Jung in the first place. In rescuing Hull from the galleys, they form the propaedeutic for a consideration of his translations, enabling one to glimpse the mode in which he understood Jung's work, and how he conceived the "task of the translator."

The following segment of correspondence between Richard Hull and Michael Fordham concerns Jung's *Psychological Types*. In his autobiography, Michael Fordham recalls: "There was another interesting episode in the editorial work, when it came to the chapter 'The type problem in poetry' in *Psychological Types*. Richard Hull wanted to restructure it so as to make the presentation more logical. I managed to show him that to do so would destroy the richness of Jung's writing. I take pride in having convinced him."[3] The correspondence shows a concern with the "question of the text" that is still so sadly lacking in Analytical Psychology. The discussion remains perhaps the most detailed textual study of the "type problem in poetry" to date. If there is one volume in Jung's oeuvre that suffers most from the neglect of close reading, while yoked to "empirical" research and a deluge of popularised simplifications, it is *Psychological Types*.

Chapter Five of *Psychological Types* consists of an extended commentary by Jung on a novel by Carl Spitteler entitled *Prometheus and Epimetheus*, and is divided into five sections: 1) Introductory remarks on Spitteler's typology, 2) A comparison of

Spitteler's with Goethe's Prometheus, 3) The significance of the uniting symbol, 4) The relativity of the symbol, and 5) The nature of the uniting symbol in Spitteler.

Hull commences by asking Fordham: "May I ask you to participate in a small experiment?" Hull's startling suggestion concerns a complete rearrangement of the narrative of text, which would place section 5) prior to section 3), thus linking the material on Spitteler. Contemporary readers may be surprised at encountering Hull's alternative version, and realizing how close this came to being the "official" version of the text. All that remains of it in the published version is an editorial note at the beginning of section 3) which suggests that "the reader may find it helpful to read the whole of section 5) at this point, as it also describes (pars. 450ff.) the fate of the redeeming symbol, the jewel whose loss was mentioned earlier (pars. 300, 310)."[4]

The correspondence that ensues takes up the intricate issue of textual autonomy and the divining of authorial intention in Jung's work. For regardless of whether one decides in favour of Hull's proposal, it is clear that it arose out of the recognition of a crucial tension within the text, which it sharply raises to the fore. In *Psychological Types* Jung elaborates his notion of *esse in anima*, which gives an ontological priority to fantasy. This, together with its independance from the functions, brings Jung's articulation of it into conflict with his concurrent attempt to develop a functional and innate typology.

As Fordham notes in his letter of 3rd December, 1965, Jung seems to assume the reader's familiarity with Spitteler. Hence, a word or two about him is in order. Spitteler was a Swiss epic and lyric poet, who was born in Liestal near Basel in 1845 and died in 1924. In 1919 he won the Nobel prize for literature, so Jung's commentary on his esteemed countryman and namesake occurred when Spitteler was at the height of his fame, and would have lent *Psychological Types* a heightened literary topicality.

Spitteler first crucially appears in Jung's work in 1912 in *Trans-formation and Symbols of the Libido*, where Jung cites him as key source for the term "imago":

> ...psychological factor which I sum up under the 'imago' has a living independance in the psychic hierarchy, i.e., possesses that autonomy which wide experience has shown to be the essential feature of feeling-toned complexes...My use of "imago" has close parallels in Spitteler's novel of the same name...In my later writings, I use the term "archetype" instead, in order to bring out the fact that we are dealing with impersonal, collective forces."[5]

Thus from the outset, Jung's notion of the autonomy of the psyche is closely bound up with his reading of Spitteler.

Spitteler's *Prometheus and Epimetheus* was first published in 1881. Jung reads the text as a revelation of the depths of the collective unconscious. While it is hard to understand how Jung claimed that it contained a "deeper truth" than Goethe's *Faust* and Nietzsche's *Zarathustra*, it is easy to see the features that would have appealed to Jung. James Muirhead notes apropos Spitteler in his translator's preface:

> In these epics he has created a mythology and a cosmogeny of his own, producing singlehandedly what it had taken generations of myth-makers to evolve. The gods and heroes of *Prometheus*...though bearing Greeks names, are new creations, sometimes showing little resemblance to their titular prototypes...While, however, adopting the usual machinery of heroes and supernal beings, Spitteler has made his myths acceptable by keeping them in close touch with the problems of common life."[6]

Spitteler would thus be one of the forgotten ancestors of today's "mythic revival." As to Spitteler's reaction to Jung's interpretation of his work, his biographer notes that he regarded the idea of a "translation" of his work into abstract psychological concepts both impossible and unnecessary.[7]

Finally, some remarks can be made concerning Hull's "experiment." Hull's strategy curiously mirrors Jung's own recommendation to the perplexed "Westerner" when faced with *The Tibetan Book of the Dead*—that one should read it backwards. Hull's experiment suggests that one may have need of similar strategies for navigating the "Bardo" of the *Collected Works*. The experiment also curiously recalls the remarkable opening section of Julio Cortazar's novel *Hopscotch*:

> In its own way, this book consists of many books, but two books above all.
>
> The first can be read in a normal fashion and it ends with Chapter 56, at the close of which there are three garish little stars which stand for the words *The End*. Consequently, the reader may ignore what follows with a clean conscience.
>
> The second should be read by beginning with Chapter 73 and then following the sequence indicated at the end of each chapter...[8]

With the verso of the text now restored, the reader is invited to partake in Hull's experiment.

Notes

1. Michael Fordham, *The Making of an Analyst*, ms., 137. For memorials to Hull, see William McGuire, "R. F. C. Hull: Recollections," *Spring* 1975, and notices by Gerhard Adler, Michael Fordham and William McGuire, *Journal of Analytical Psychology*, Vol. 21 no. 1, 1976.
2. For an account of the editing of the *Collected Works*, see William McGuire, *Bollingen. An adventure in collecting the past* (Princeton: Princeton University Press, 1982).
3. Michael Fordham, *The Making of an Analyst*, ms., 134.
4. *CW* 6, footnote to § 318.
5. *CW* 5, § 62, footnote 5. The last sentence quoted here was an addition to the 1952 *Symbols of Transformation*. Spitteler's *Imago* appeared in 1906. A brief summary of it, together with a description of its reception by the early psy-

choanalysts, is given by Ellenberger, in *The Discovery of the Unconscious*, (New York: Basic Books, 1970), 794-5. Ellenberger also suggests that it forms the source of Jung's notion of the anima.

6. "Prefatory note by translator," Carl Spitteler, *Prometheus and Epimetheus. A prose epic*, tr. James Muirhead, (London: Jarrolds, 1931) 12. Jung seems not to have been alone in the comparison of Spitteler with Goethe and Nietzsche, as evidenced by Muirhead's article "Carl Spitteler and the Epic Novel," in *Essays by Diverse Hands — transactions of the Royal Society of Literature*, 1932.

7. Werner Stauffacher, *Carl Spitteler, Biographie* (Zürich: Artemis Verlag, 1973), 610. Stauffacher also notes that there is a copy of *Psychological Types* bearing Jung's dedication in Spitteler's literary remains. Jung was apparently aware of Spitteler's reaction. In 1936 he said:

> Spitteler was too much possessed by the figures of the background, his ego was woven into them and his descriptions are too exuberant and spun out. This happens when there is not enough objectivity. Spitteler was exceedingly angry at the idea that his work could be symbolical, or that it had any significance beyond his actual intention. He said he could just as easily have written a song "May is here," if he had been so disposed. Artists are often exceedingly resentful of the idea that their work does not consist entirely of the foreground which they have spun out of their conscious resources. (E.T.H. seminar, 12th June 1936, 4.)

8. Julio Cortazar, *Hopscotch*, tr. Gregory Rabassa, (New York: Pantheon, 1966).

Acknowledgment.

The originals of the letters are in the possession of Michael Fordham and Birthe-Lena Hull, whom I thank for assistance in preparation, and for permission to publish.

*Brief references to other editorial matters in Hull to Fordham, 27th October 1965
and 27th November 1965, have been omitted, as indicated by three dots. Hull's
letter of 27th October 1965 also contains some marginal annotations by Fordham,
which have not been reproduced, as the points are taken up in his letter of 29th
October, 1965.*

{Hull to Fordham:}

27 October 1965

Dear Michael,

May I ask you to participate in a small experiment? Would you read
through the enclosed pages [Marginal note: "Under Separate Cover".
Ed.], which represent ch. V of Psychological Types, with particular attention to the arrangement of the Spitteler material, and then look at
the Baynes version,{1} which follows the original order?

As you will see, I have placed section 5 of the original, "The Nature
of the Uniting Symbol in Spitteler," immediately after section 2, "A
Comparison of Spitteler's with Goethe's Prometheus," and followed it
with the introduction to the original section 3, "The Significance of the
Uniting Symbol" (Baynes, pp. 234-242). In this way all the Spitteler
material is brought together and presented as an independent chapter,
which is rounded off with the paragraph that concluded ch. V in Baynes (p. 336). The remaining sections of the original, 3a-d and 4a-b, each
form a separate chapter.

I suggest this arrangement partly because sections 3a-d and 4a-b have
nothing to do with poetry, the theme of ch. V, but chiefly because section 2 repeatedly anticipates explanations which are only given in section 5. For example, the reference on p. 249 (end) of the typescript
(Baynes p. 228 end and 229 top) to the pact with Behemoth and to the
divine children, and on p. 255 (Baynes p. 234) to the pact with evil, remains incomprehensible until the story of Behemoth and the children
is recounted a hundred pages later (pp. 357ff.; Baynes pp. 333ff.). Again,
the reference to the loss of the jewel (p. 243, Baynes p. 222) is explained
only on pp. 353ff. (Baynes pp. 329ff.). Similarly, section 5 refers back
to details in 2, which by that time the reader may well have forgotten.
Another point of importance is that the introduction to "The Significance of the Uniting Symbol" (pp. 255-262, Baynes pp. 234-242) reads
like a recapitulation and general criticism of the Spitteler material, as
though serving rather to sum up this whole section than to introduce a

new one. Further, by presenting sections 3a-d and 4a-b as separate chapters, due prominence is given to the concept of the uniting symbol.

Besides the division into three chapters and the regrouping of the Spitteler material, I'd like to draw attention to the passage on 292-5 (Baynes pp. 269-272). This excursus on Parsifal (mentioned only once before, Baynes p. 239) seems to have very little connection with Taoist symbolism. The "primordial image" in question can hardly be tao, except in the very general sense that tao unites the male-female opposites among others. But it does have a direct connection with the vas-uterus symbolism symbolized by the Grail, which is discussed on pp. 313ff. (Baynes pp. 290 ff. Tentatively, therefore, I have inserted this passage towards the end of section 4a, where it introduces the discussion of the derivation of symbols not from repressed sexuality but from archaic residues, and forms a link with section 4b, where the Grail legend is taken up again.

I have discussed these proposed rearrangements with Gerhard {Adler}, and though he agrees that they present the material in a more logical order and clarify the exposition he is not in favor of them, on the ground that Jung left ch. V unchanged throughout the new editions for 40 years, including the Ges. Werke edition of 1960. He is, however, quite willing that I should raise the matter with you and ask for your opinion. He also agrees that Jung might well have authorized such a rearrangement (as he did in other cases) had he been alive. If you feel there is a good case for a "linear presentation" as opposed to the famous "circular thinking," thus considerably easing the task of the student, please would you discuss it with Gerhard when he returns? Another point to be considered is the conformity of the paragraph numbering with the G. W. edition. Gerhard suggests that if long paragraphs are broken up they should be numbered a-b-c etc. This has been done nowhere before in our edition, though of course there would be no objection to it on that score...

...Looking forward to hearing from you, and with best regards,

Yours sincerely,

Richard

{Fordham to Hull:}

29th October, 1965

Dear Richard,

A letter like that puts me on the spot because I spent a lot of my time editing papers for the Journal doing with them what you want to do with Jung. ~~and~~ If you had been let loose on his writings earlier I am sure there would have been a lot more Jungians about than there are now! However, I agree with Gerhard that we should withhold our editorial 'good sense.'

Quite recently I have been reading through the essays in volume 13 and getting quite mad with the way Jung jumps about even in these. It does nothing to ~~help~~ further his thesis and confuses the reader. As I understand it all this is due to Jung plunging himself into active imagination—~~and~~ the carnage of it gets reflected in his writings. This by the way was noticed by Avis Dry.{2} We could be justified in tidying up if Jung had not said that his writings are a self-expression, and it is useful to have the varying degrees of order and disorder recorded so that these can be correlated with the account given in Memories Dreams and Reflections and probably other publications to appear later.

There is a compromise I think which we might ~~imply~~ try: it is to put in editorial footnotes, cross-referencing pages you cite. The reader who wants to fill in the gaps can do so more easily and I will discuss this with Gerhard.

As you evidently like doing this kind of work would you consider looking at a collection of my papers - my more recent publications and issues - to think of ways of making them into a book, or if you cannot, to tell me how to make a book out of the ideas in them?

Best wishes,
Yours,
Michael

{Hull to Fordham:}

2 November

...PS Your letter has just arrived - best thanks. Yes of course: at the time Jung was writing TYPES he was going through old harry with his unconscious, as we know from the autobiography. But I wonder whether part of the "carnage" in this book and elsewhere is due not so much to active imagination as to his peculiar method of composition. Jung's lack of systematization is often excused (or condemned) as "circular thinking," but if one examines the manuscripts one sees that he didn't think circularly at all. In the case of the Mysterium, for instance, the theme of each chapter is developed in a perfectly logical, "linear" way first of all, and then come innumerable insertions, and insertions within insertions, pages long, of amplificatory and illustrative material, so that when at last he picks up the thread again he has to recapitulate some point in the previous argument. It is this that gives the impression of "circularity." Besides this, I found several instances where the typist slipped up and put an insertion in the wrong place, or where Jung had keyed an insertion into two different places! Naturally I don't pretend that this could have happened to section 5 of ch. V of TYPES, but I think it may very well have happened to the passage about the Grail: it could have found its way accidentally to the end of the wrong chapter. There is absolutely nothing in the Chinese material about sexuality. I would therefore plead very ardently for its transfer to section 4a. I have tried to get hold of the MS. but without success. As to section 5, well, if this rather obvious little bit of tidying up would spare the reader irritation and even win adherents to the cause, wouldn't that be doing Jung a service?

I do like doing this kind of work, certainly, and would be very happy to look at a collection of your papers.

Best wishes,
R.

{Fordham to Hull:}

24th November, 1965

Dear Richard,

'The type problem in poetry' was a at one time a much admired and much puzzled-about piece. I remember distinctly that I repeatedly got bogged down in the passages about Behemoth and the divine children and even the second more explanatory passage did not help very much until I discovered a second-hand copy of Muirhead's translation.

On re-reading my Baynes, which I had not looked at for many years, I was gratified to find quite sensible and helpful pencil marks which

made me understand where I had got the sense of the chapter and
where I had got lost.

It is, as you rightly imply, a most indigestible proposition and I am
not sure that even now I have truly mastered it and understood why
Jung wrote it like this. Howevere as it stands it is coherent and in line
with the method Jung uses elsewhere - most in Symbols and Mysterium. He takes a text and uses it as a basis to expatiate upon. Is not that
one reason why he has returned in the last section to Spitteler?

I would infer that his idea was as follows:-

1) Start with Spitteler and show how extraversion and introversion are
loked at by an introvert.

2) Compare with Goethe (an extravert) and see how he works on the
same problem. Then suggest an interpretation of their solutions.

3) Extract problem of opposites for excursus on eastern mysticism and
the way they are dealt with by the eastern mystics. End with a link to a
western solution (Parsifal).

4)Take up the soul question, indicated at the start, and then the relation of the soul to God as a western development.

5) End up with Spitteler to give coherence to the seemingly lost theme,
i.e. Spitteler (and Goethe secondarily) on types as manifestation of opposites.

In line with this view, it is understandable why "The significance of
the uniting symbol" "reads like a recapitulation and general criticism of
the Spitteler material." It is because he is now going to leave it for 78
pages and so he wants to "sum up this whole section".

I think this is a feasible, if not the correct reading of what was in
Jung's mind. It agrees with your thesis that his writings have a linear
coherence. Certainly Jung's thinking is not circular - it can be diffuse
and disjunctive but I have never noticed circularity - where, by the
way, did this idea come from? I have come across it once or twice but
never thought it was a serious proposition.

I think we have to recognize that this chapter has much more of the
eruptive element in it - deriving from active imagination - than the others and is of interest just for that reason.

Now to turn to your more specific points. Jung's habit of hinting at
one point and taking it up in more detail later on is characteristic. He
once expatiated on this to me and it has often helped in understanding
his writing. He said that he put out a hint so that it could germinate in

the readers' minds. Some would notice it, think about it so that when he took it up later some readers will already have an idea with which to meet the later exposition. You may say that it does not come off if there are 100 pages between the two and I shall agree with you, but we are here to edit Jung in the light of what we know of him.

Likewise his habit of making jumps without explaining himself is, I agree, disconcerting, c.f. your relevant objection to the excursus on Parisfal in connection with Taoism. I would think that the answer lies on p. 98 (Baynes) where Jung fills in the gap (171 pages! - worse and worse for the student you may say and with truth!).

I should be unfair if I did not say that though I think your arrangement interesting and has stimulated me a good deal as you can see, I think that it introduces chapters with virtually no reference to types in them. I could only wish this were a book on the dynamic relation between introversion and extraversion rather than a book on types, but it is not and the reconciling symbol has therefore to be almost smuggled in through poets as Jung does. Finally you say that eastern mysticism and the service of the soul is not poetry - I am not so sure, but am no poet!

This letter is sent direct to you and its contents have not been seen by Gerhard because I want to hear what you think without making it all into an editorial issue. All the same as you say my conclusion is the same as his but on different grounds.

Best wishes,

Yours,

Michael

{Hull to Fordham:}

27 November 1965

Dear Michael,

I was very glad to have your long and interesting letter on ch. V of TYPES. Your exposition of the rationale of this chapter seems to me to be perfectly feasible and I have no doubt it is a correct interpretation. The slight rearrangement I have proposed, however, does nothing to damage the actual structure of the chapter; on the contrary, I would claim that the structure is thereby reinforced as regards both the presentation of the material and its psychological interpretation. To take the most obvious example, the opening words of section 3 (Baynes p. 234): "If from the standpoint now gained..." But we have gained no new standpoint as regards the "compact with evil," first mentioned out of the blue on p. 228/9 as the "compact with Behemoth and his evil host." We have no idea what this compact is, and we do not know the role of Epimetheus in it. This is explained only at the end of section 5. In your rationale you say of this section: "End up with Spitteler to give coherence to the seemingly lost theme, i. e. Spitteler (and Goethe secondarily) on types as manifestation of opposites." In other words, if I understand you correctly, you correlate the material in this section with the problem of opposites as represented by Spitteler's attitude-types, and as resolved by the reconciling symbol. Of orig. section 3 you say: "Extract problem of opposites for excursus on eastern mysticism." Now, by placing section 5 before section 3, it seems to me that we kill three birds with one stone:

1) We put the story of Behemoth and the pact with evil in its proper context, so that we really have gained a new standpoint when we come to orig. section 3.

2) We have retrieved the "seemingly lost theme:" Spitteler's attitude-types.

3) We have placed the problem of opposites represented by this theme where it serves as a comprehensive introduction to the excursus on eastern mysticism and on the reconciling symbol.

In case you didn't take a copy of your letter, I recapitulate your rationale and correlate it with the section headings (p. refs. to Baynes). It was merely a proposition to divide the chapter into three parts, thus introducing, as you say, new chapters with no reference to types in the headings (more about this later). The original structure as a single chapter could still be preserved:

1. Introductory Remarks on Spitteler's Characterization of Types

[Start with Spitteler and show how extraversion and introversion are looked at by an introvert.]

2. A Comparison of Spitteler's with Goethe's Prometheus

[Compare with Goethe (an extravert) and see how he works on the same problem. Then suggest an interpretation of their solutions.]

3. The Nature of the Uniting Symbol in Spitteler (p. 319 par. 2 - p. 336 minus last par.)

[Your rationale of orig. 5, modified: Spitteler's attitude-types (extraversion and introversion) as illustration of the conflict of opposites reconciled by the symbol: "soul's jewel" = "saviour," etc.]

4. The Significance of the Uniting Symbol (p. 234 - 242)

[My rationale: Recapitulation and general criticism of Spitteler material.]

5. The Uniting Symbol of Eastern Religion (p. 242 - 269)

[Illustrate problem of opposites by excursus on eastern mysticism.]

6. The Relativity of the Symbol

a) Service of Woman and the Soul (p. 272-297 + 269-272 [Parsifal])

b) Meister Eckhart (p. 297-319 par. 1 + 336 last par.)

[Take up the soul question, indicated at the start, and then the relation of the soul to God as a western development. Period. End of chapter.]

In your rationale you take the Parsifal passage as a link to a western solution of the problem of opposites. This is undoubtedly true, but one has to *work* to get that link! It is nowhere explicitly stated to be such; it is presented as an incongruous appendix to Taoism. By placing it at the end of 6a above, we put it in the context of the historical material (Grail symbolism) and of the psychological interpretation of this symbolism (derivation from archetypal engrams). The passage is still a link, but the link is in its proper place.

The division into three chapters, as originally proposed, was designed also to give prominence to the concept of the uniting symbol. (This, by the way, is the only change in Jungian terminology I regret. "Reconciling symbol" is so much more emotive I would withdraw this division in order to keep the chapter whole and to avoid introducing chapters whose headings, unlike all the others, do not refer specifically to the type problem. But I would question your view that the reconciling symbol has to be "smuggled in through the poets" because this is a book on *types* rather than on the dynamic relation between introversion and extraversion. It depends very much on what you mean by "types." The book, as I see it, is fundamentally about *attitude types* and only secondarily about *function types*. The function types are, so to speak, mere exponents of introversion and extraversion. Indeed ch. X, "General Description of the Types," is expressly organized on the division between the extraverted type and the introverted type, the "general types," while the function types are called "special types."

(Baynes, p. 412; see also first par. on p. 9). In the genesis of Jung's ideas, wouldn't you say, the concept of introversion and extraversion definitely comes before that of the function types; the original two functions, thinking and feeling, are more like expressions or even mere concomitants of the movement of libido. This comes out particularly clearly in the Jung-Schmid correspondence{3}: they get to abusing each other not as "thinkers" and "feelers" - for it is admitted that introverts *can* feel and extraverts think, even if badly - but as incorrigible introverts and extraverts. You can change your function with luck, but you're stuck with your attitude for life! I send you the translation of this correspondence, as I'm sure you'll find it amusing as well as instructive in all sorts of ways. The copy is not yet corrected as there are some queries for Gerhard, so please bear with any obscurities.

This is no doubt an academic point so far as the organization of ch. V is concerned, but I do hope you will give further consideration to this new grouping of the sections. TYPES is supposed to be Jung's classic; anything that aids clarity for, we hope, generations of students to come is surely to the good? If even you got bogged down on first studying this chapter and are not sure even now that you understand why Jung wrote it like this, Lord help the innocent student! It took me six months' work on the book to get a clearer grasp of its basic cohesion, the details of which, I would maintain, are sometimes obscured less by design than by inadvertence. You concede that Jung's thinking has a "linear coherence" and is not "circular," a euphemism in most cases for muddled. (They take this circularity very seriously in Zürich. If you don't think circular, you're nothing, a rationalizing victim of mere logic. The mystique of circularity justifies every sloppiness in argument and presentation.) Finally, to edit Jung, or any author, in the light of what one knows of him means making use of a highly differential criterion. So much depends on who "one" is and what "one" knows! The two combined reinforce a personal equation which may be at odds with another person's equally subjective (or, as he will claim) objective view of the same material. Thus you know the value of Jung's "discontinuous" exposition, a characteristic that was often quite deliberate, whereas I value his no less deliberate linear coherence. To strike a balance between the two is very difficult...

With best regards,
Richard

Fordham to Hull :
3rd December 1965
Dear Hull,

I am much enjoying this correspondence and want to continue somewhat further with it.

First about the 'standpoint gained'. I admit difficulty in finding it, but surely it is that of the 'medieval magician' who represents an element 'still untouched by the christian cleavage' and who can therefore be the carrier of the reconciling symbol since evil has not got the same absoluteness developed by Christains. I would see in this the beginning of Jung's enthusiasm for alchemy of which he does not seem to have been sufficiently certain at that time.

The trouble about the divine children and 'the compact with Behemoth and his evil host' was not soluble to me until I read the Spitteler material. I concluded that it arose from Jung's assumption that the reader is familiar with Spitteler. Once one has looked at the book all becomes clear and one stops thinking in terms of the Bible! You may reply that it was only because I picked up the volume by chance in a second hand book shop that I am clear now - and you would say this with justice that I might have gone to the B. M.! However you have, I think, implied a possible solution: a footnote giving the relevant details from Spitteler and referring the reader to the later passage.

I fully admit the persuasiveness of your arrangement which appears to me personally, though not as editor. Incidentally, it brings to light another feature of this chapter which may have something to do with this tireless seemingly silly and nefariously used argument about circularity. Circularity is a characteristic of affective processes (circumambulation) and not thought. Your remark about Zurich amplifies for me the muddle, defensive evasions of real issues, infantile outbursts, and obstinancy of which I have had plenty!

There are two elements in Jung's thesis. First there is the collective unconscious idea which makes it possible to ignore differences due to history and geography, physics, chemistry, etc. and extract the common factor (the archetype); second there are the differences which are used in varying ways. There is no difficulty I take it about the geography (east and west) but I think it is worth noting that there is temporal arrangement.

Early sections on Spitteler	18th & 19th centuries
& Goethe	predominantly
Sections on Hermes	2nd century
Section on Eckehard	13th century
Final section	18th & 19th centuries
	again.

Thus there is a sort of circle involved resulting from, logically speaking, the condensation of two theses.

Your remarks about editing contain two issues. You are wrong in thinking that I appreciate Jung's 'discontinuities' which I think are often due to concelaed thought disorders (!) and I wish that the logical linear coherence of his argument too often left implicit had often been made more explicit. I also agree with what you say about editing but our conclusions are different. It is because of the 'subjective' factor that I am not in favour of making textual changes except when it can be shown that the typist or such like has been muddling things up. I think on the other hand that editorial notes can be used to clarify obscure points and I don't see why this could not be done with this chapter.

My understanding of types is as follows: C. G. defined six variables (two attitudes and four functions). This makes a rather formidable number of possible combinations restricted by the incompatibilities on the basis of which he could describe 8 types (cf. general descriptions of them). He defines a type by the predominatingly conscious attitude and function. True, as you say, each type can display the other attitudes, functions (inferior attitudes and functions). This was driven home to me once when Baynes used to tell me I needed to work at my 'inferior feeling' and this made me think angrily that he was a fool!

Yes I think that introversion and extraversion is put first in this volume because he might have described the types under functions, i.e. four main types with two, extraverted and introverted, subsidiary attitudes. In view of the later importance he attaches to the four this arrangement would have been logical - but he did not do this.

I believe Jung considered that a type was basically irreversible and linked to hereditary predisposition. A book on types does imply this and so should be emphasised rather than the symbolic solution between opposites. Strictly speaking if types are reconcilable they are not types in the above sense but a way of describing aspects of one self. This at any rate was the source of my idea that the reconciling (uniting) symbol had to be 'smuggled in through the poets'. Otherwise it tends to undermine the typological idea. It is for this reason that I think that your division which aims to give 'due prominence to the concept of the uniting symbol' may give undue prominence to it...

Yours,

Michael

EDITOR'S NOTES TO THE LETTERS

1. The reference is to H. G. Baynes' translation of *Psychological Types* (London: Kegan Paul, Trench, Trubner, 1923).

2. The reference is to Avis Dry, *The psychology of Jung: a critical interpretation* (London: Methuen, 1961).

3. The Jung-Schmid letters, which throw an incomparable light upon the genesis of Jung's thinking on psychological types, have been published in German. See Hans Konrad Iselin, *Zur Enstehung von C. G. Jungs 'Psychologischen Typen'. Der Briefwechsel zwischen C. G. Jung und Hans Schmid-Guisan in Lichte ihrer Freundschaft* (Frankfurt-am-Main: Verlag Sauerlander, 1982).

WHIPPING THE CHTHONIC WOMAN

SHEILA GRIMALDI-CRAIG

Claire Douglas, *Translate This Darkness, The Life of Christiana Morgan.*
New York, Simon & Schuster, 1993. Pp. 398. $25.00, cloth.

There is one theme that sounds through this book like the Titanic's
foghorn: an inspiring woman is catastrophically wasting her life when
she plays nothing more than a muse in the lives of accomplished men.
On page after page the author pours her scorn for a psychoanalytic
theory that supported such a role, and her contempt for the men who,
in her view, were its blind, cruel, arrogant beneficiaries. (On the cover
May Sarton offers the usual rallying cry: "This is a book for anyone
capable of anger and frustration at male arrogance and for women who
deem themselves to be used.")

The *femme inspiratrice* is Christiana Morgan (1897-1967), whose life,
along with her Romantic soul-mate Harry Murray's, I celebrated in
SPRING 54 in my review of Forrest Robinson's *Love's Story Told, A
Life of Henry A. Murray.* The accomplished men are no less than C. G.
Jung, Alfred North Whitehead, Harry Murray, Chaim Weizmann,
Lewis Mumford, and others. The author is Claire Douglas, a Jungian
analyst.

Sheila Grimaldi-Craig taught for many years in the Connecticut Public
Schools. She describes herself as "just an old-fashioned dame with old-fashioned
values."

The author presents such a compelling picture of the beautiful, imaginative, long-suffering Christiana, and such a repellent picture of the great men in her life, that one realizes just how powerful Christiana Morgan's gift for inspiration really is. But Claire Douglas despises the role of woman as inspiratrice (for men) even as she lets it take hold of her own judgment.

Since I already told you who Christiana Morgan was in the last issue (a Boston socialite who in the 1920s analyzed with Jung, painting pictures of her psychological state that became the subject of Jung's later Visions Seminars—a practicing analyst, with her secret lover, Harry Murray, at Harvard's Psychologal Clinic, in the 1930s, 40s and 50s, where they developed together [itself a sore point with Claire Douglas who wants Christiana to get more credit] the famous Thematic Apperception Test—and an American sexual adventurer of the first rank) we'll skip going through all that again.

In her early years, Christiana was a sexual fireball (even in her sixties Harvard professors dismissed her, says Douglas, as nothing but a nymphomaniac) who went around turning the wimpy men in her life onto Nietzsche's *The Will to Power*. For the most part, Douglas doesn't approve of Christiana's sexual indulgences, and she certainly has no use for her advocacy of Nietzsche. Christiana often attacked her husband, Bill, for his "weakness and lack of vigor" (he died at age forty from tuberculosis contracted in the trenches of World War I). Douglas finds it odd that Christiana, excited by men, liked the sexuality of power games: "Unable to understand why she failed to respond, he sought to prove his manliness to her and to himself through admiration of his returning physical strength and, perhaps above all else, in claiming that Christiana's sexuality was proof of his power over her. The odd thing is that the virile chest-beating excited Christiana, and although Bill was not hero enough for her, she took these violent expressions of power as a proof of his manliness. She wrote to him demanding that he tell her how he loved her, that he thrill her and make her afraid."

She was, at the same time, having an affair with men of intellectual power, including Chaim Weizmann, who later became the first president of Israel, and with them, too, she pushed Nietzsche's book. Douglas presents Christiana's Nietzschean yearnings for power (and to be overpowered) as foolish, because she was wasting precious female sexuality in a male ideology. In Douglas' late 20th-century eyes, Bill and Christiana's marriage needed "reality rather than the heroic Nietzschean bombast that disguised them from themselves and from each other."

But what would reality for Christiana Morgan look like if it wouldn't contain the tubercular Bill, whom Douglas sees as trying to hold his wife "to traditional notions of marriage," and if there would be no use for the Nietzschean woman, which is what started this good upperclass Boston girl wanting to explore the depths of life in the first place?

If Christiana Morgan were alive in the late 20th century, she'd be listening to hard core bands, checking out porn videos, and writing a very different kind of book from the academic "research" papers she and Harry took so seriously once upon a time. Let's face it: she'd be a Madonna with brains (if she had a little more humor), and she'd insist that anti-Romantic, anti-Sadean, and anti-sexual feminists leave her life story alone and make their own.

Reality is everyone's convenient word for their own agitprop, and in spite of all the teeth-gnashing over how Christiana was wasting her life, Claire Douglas never does say what she should have done instead. (There is a passage about what would happen if a woman like Christiana came to a good woman therapist today, how differently, and more sensitively, things would be done.)

The same idealizing one-sidedness covers all Christiana's sexual affairs here as Douglas screens them: so while Harry Murray's (betraying) affairs with other women are always reprehensible and "serious," the author always forgives Christiana for hers because they are routine and never really "serious."

"Christiana, along with many of her iconoclastic generation and class, had felt free to take other lovers and experience other entanglements, but they had always been secondary to her love for Harry. She soon realized, however, that his affair with Eleanor was far more serious." This disclaimer comes as we read of Christiana's affair with one Ralph Eaton, a young Harvard student who becomes her lover and then, abandoned when he gets too "serious," commits suicide on her property. Christiana "...decided she had treated their affair too lightly."

There are more affairs and heartbreaks, recriminations and tragic deaths in this book than in a month of *All My Children*. And just as with "Erica Kane" on the soap—who's done everyone and been everything—Christiana is always portrayed here as the suffering woman, enduring a wasted, neglected, abused (but oh so privileged) life.

Notwithstanding the feminist lens through which everything is examined in this book, Douglas presents a rousing critique of Jung's analysis of Christiana Morgan. In this, Douglas, like John Kerr, Richard Noll and Sonu Shamdasani in other areas, is breaking new ground. It's about time Jungians cut through some of the over-idealized vapors and Zurich pieties that sanctify their founder to this day.

Christiana was 28 when she went to Jung to be analyzed. Douglas presents the relationship Jung had with Toni Wolff, whereby Emma Jung and Toni—wife and mistress—had to adjust to his schedule for them in his life, as the model Jung used in treating Christiana. "From his relationship with Toni Wolff, Jung understood that Christiana Morgan lacked comprehension not only of her own passionate earthiness but also of the spiritual side of her sexuality. Wolff had awakened Jung to these two sides of women's sexuality, and through it they experienced a doubly potent conjugation; Jung recognized that Christiana and Harry might be capable of a similar union. Jung also realized that she was confronting one of the major dilemmas of the age: how to be responsibly alive to all aspects of herself without restriction. The religious aspect in her erotic conflict and behind her love for Harry might lead her beyond Christianity's denial and repression to a far more perilous and complex integration of the body and of evil."

But how could a man—even Jung—truly liberate a woman? Douglas faults the man—men—and the age itself. "Yet at the same time, the very fact that Christiana Morgan was a woman blinded Jung to many of her possibilities. Neither his understanding of women's psychology, nor his conflicted attitude toward his own mother, nor the era itself could allow for a really autonomous woman. Jung knew that he and his patient were struggling with a similar problem but, rather than viewing her as his counterpart, he instructed Morgan to live her life very much in the same way Toni Wolff lived hers—as adjunct to and in the service of her lover...In moments like these, and they were many, Jung forgot Christiana Morgan while he glorified her role as an anima figure and inspiratrice for a man. Jung's anti-therapeutic, nineteenth-century masculine lens could only see women fulfilling themselves through fulfilling men's needs."

Given this premise, one must conclude that all Jung's analyses of women were bad analyses. "Jung's analysis of Christiana Morgan," Douglas says, "constitutes almost a primer of what a good and a bad analysis involves. Though Jung could not have been more helpful to her in his interpretations and support concerning many of her problems, and although his warmth, deep interest, and liking for her were healing, the analysis faltered when Jung's own complexes and the cultural norms of the time interfered and became arbiters of psychological health."

But aren't "the norms of the time" pretty much the whole issue here? This would be an unusual book if it was written by a contemporary of Jung, or by Christiana Morgan herself. It's something else written decades later. Should Jung have told Christiana to go it alone—be an Emily Dickinson of waking dreams? But Christiana was no poet, and her paintings—made famous by Jung himself as illustrations of the female psyche—are not very promising as "art." Why not the Toni Wolff model? Unless you have more confidence than I do in Toni Wolff's own potential for true and original greatness, she still seems an extremely fortunate woman to have been able to hitch her mediocre wagon to Jung's blazing star. What did Christiana have to recommend her at the time as some potentially great future psychologist of womanhood? The only thing she had produced at this point was a diploma from a wretched finishing school (and that just barely) and a five year old son.

It may be true (if rather conveniently so) that potentially great but not quite successful women have underachieved because they settled for the *inspiratrice* role instead of betting on themselves. Underachieving men might argue the converse (they don't dare!): they didn't concentrate enough on themselves but spent too much time talking to the *inspiratrice* wife. We all know about wishful thinking and self-victimization and how much "the age" can be blamed.

It's perhaps kind of Douglas to blame "the age" at least in part—it's not *entirely* Jung's fault. But does Jung need this excuse? To be sure, there are probably more analysts out there today telling women patients to inspire themselves and not waste their talent on men—but there must be some (and not just the male ones) who would still give Jung's advice in the same situation (assuming analysts still *give advice* as they did in the old days).

But Jung is the enemy here (for Douglas) clearly because his advice to Christiana seems so self-serving: "Warning her that she needed a strong 'ego stance' from which to face her visions, he encouraged her to steady herself by giving form to the visions in her art as he had done, but also to remain centered in her responsibilities to her husband, her child, and her possible relationship to Harry." On the face of it, this doesn't sound like bad advice. You have to be a Romantic of a different sort to argue that she should have been told to go for it all right then—throw those bourgeois anchors overboard and plunge into the female depths—what Douglas likes to call "the chthonic feminine."

But Christiana's visions were extraordinary, tremendously self-enriching. They were so extraordinary that Douglas claims they unhinged Jung. Thus, when Christiana develops her spectacular visions under Jung's guidance, Douglas says Jung became caught in counter-transference of an unusual kind: "He had known that she was going through a process similar to his own, but now he realized that she was doing it in a passionate feminine way. It was as if he were seeing an alternative world full of dynamic images that simultaneously excited and repelled him; they caught him between erotic attraction for their discoverer and a need to dismiss her power."

Here the book is on new ground. After all, when it comes to gender prejudice, every man is guilty anyway (as now more and more women are). So it is good to have Douglas's attack on Jung out in the open for once and for him to come in for his share of criticism. "Jung was thrilled with her vision book but, alas, responded as a man rather than an analyst."

And Douglas can really work you up into a state about it: "Jung now started to sound jealous...The tragedy of what happened next, as much a product of the culture as of Jung's personality, was a circumstance that has been too often repeated in the analysis of women. Jung did not know how to deal with the power he had helped unleash; he began to view his patient primarily as a woman, and his traditional gender prejudices overpowered all psychological observations...Men faced with this feminine power tend to flee, or to combat it by seizing it for themselves, trying to surmount it through lovemaking or rape."

But wait a minute. What was it that Jung did that was so bad, so male-prejudiced, so 19th-century theory bound, so fugal and tragic? *He told her not to forget to use her mind!* Just when the going gets good, and

Christiana is really down in the depths of her feminine psyche, the terra nova of the "chthonic feminine," Jung calls a halt. He does so by reminding her to *think*. Thinking is of course the other side of the feeling function that is itself either a) a good thing (for feminists) if seen as women's special gift in contrast with most men or b) a bad thing if seen as what women do as opposed to most men (who think). The thinking/feeling function in Jungian theory is feminist dynamite, and Douglas blows off a few caps of the stuff. In this instance, she manages to put a bad spin on thinking.

"'You were living the life which had hitherto been unconscious,' Jung tells Christiana, 'and this seems as though it could go on forever. It is a great renewal of life and energy. It is a wonderful flowing. But at the same time...to grow you must also use your mind. If you only flow then you only reach a deep level where there is no tension—all levels become the same.'"

The way he wanted her to think here was to deepen and relativize the experiences she was having by seeing them in some kind of context (but of course all contexts are inevitably male-gender prejudiced, so Jung loses this one, too). He wanted her to know the mythic parallels to her visions. At this point in her analysis, Christiana was bubbling over with visions, on fire with herself. Should Jung remind her that these visions are not just hers, but part of a past history of the human race that involves everyone in the world? (Then he's co-opting the chthonic feminine's visions for men's imperialistic view of history.) What Douglas sees as Jung's jealousy (that they were not his visions) is fascinating: but of course they were his visions in one sense—they were everyone's visions. Christiana was making a valuable contribution to the human psyche, at least if you believe there is such a thing as the *human* psyche.

To insist that this should have been seen as primarily a contribution to the psyche of women, and only then to the rest of the human race, is the issue. To see Jung, wanting her to relativize it into a historic context, as doing her (and women) a disservice, is one of the first shots off the starboard bow in the war of feminist Jungian revisionism. It's not exactly a shot heard round the world (or even as far as Zurich, perhaps) but it needs to be fired and this book deserves a lot of credit.

It's hard to put down, and well researched (although the Fugitives were a literary group at Vanderbilt in Tennessee, certainly not at Black

Mountain College in North Carolina, which notoriously abhorred Southern agrarian poets, and Christiana's colleague, the poet Merrill Moore, went to Vanderbilt, not Black Mountain, which he never would have laid eyes on in a coon's age—the author is confusing Moore with Harry's friend, the poet Charles Olson, who taught at Black Mountain in the 1950s).

There is nonetheless this lingering question of whether we—several decades later (and would it be any different in the same year?) can read an ongoing analysis (the patient's notes no less) on a day by day basis and criticize the analyst for it. For instance: one day Jung apparently tells her Harry is immature and flighty. Another day: "You must become more of a woman." This is seen (by Douglas) as "assailing her for what he had formerly encouraged," (that is, telling her to use her mind.) "Christiana's visions were making her a woman, but one too large and complex to fit into the confines of tradition's female shell."

Well, maybe so. But the same could be said of Jung's analysis of men, too. He didn't seem to do all that much for some rich American men either, like Medill McCormick (see *Spring 50*). And Harry Murray himself, though he felt very positive about his relationship with Jung, was always an unfinished sort of man, too (what man isn't?). Or is tradition's male shell so complete and full that Douglas is satisfied with it? (I know, the triumph of feminism will liberate men too.) Certainly now, after several further decades of imagining what a woman can be, it is easy to say that Christiana was a potentially bigger woman than what Jung saw in her—and he saw a lot . But the fact that she became a big enough woman for us to be paying attention to her life in this way does say something about her life too.

I suppose the real issue is, did he hinder her? Did he stop her in any way from being all that she could be. Was this indeed a bad analysis? Did its losses outweigh its gains? Douglas' portrait of Jung in this analysis is of a jealous, blustering "Siegfried," whose tone is "not only hostile but coarsely brutal, as if everything of value were male and could be obtained through the masculine ...whipping his patient with her animus," and whose "...reaction to the daemonic feminine was no longer to flee it or destroy it but to seize its energy for himself."

"You are like Brunnhilde," Siegfried Jung tells this "chthonic feminine" volcano of a patient. "You have never been broken in."

It's amazing stuff. And Chrstiana, according to Douglas, was painting a larger mythical canvas than anything conceived by Zurich Niebelungs: "Toward the end of her visions book, in February 1927, she discovered what the masculine era had tried to hide: that not only the primitive and spiritual feminine needed uniting, but also the masculine figures of Satan and Christ...She raised this Satanic Christ up out of her own unconscious, and as it surfaced, the Judeo-Christian world crumbled beneath her...The masculine Satanic Christ firmly in consciousness, she embarked again on another powerful series of ascents and descents. This stunning vision prefigured and may well have inspired Jung's important theoretical work on the same subject in 'Answer to Job,' while the visions as a whole anticipate Jung's final work, *Mysterium Coniunctionis: An Inquiry into the Separation and Synthesis of Psychic Opposites in Alchemy.*"

In Douglas' view, Jung was never able to grasp the importance of Christiana's dragon, the chthonic feminine with whom she made peace instead of killing à la Siegfried and the traditional male hero. Had he done so, Douglas argues, it would have been "a leap ahead for Jung's antiquated theories of a wounded, pallid, mourning feminine."

If left entirely to Jung, Christiana Morgan would have been just another one of the many women Jung shaped to his mold and convenience. Douglas doesn't like the other women who were around Jung in the 20s—she says Jung reveled in the Morgans' "... graceful, light humor and their effect on the more somber members of the Zurich group." Christiana "...caused quite a stir among the solemn 'handmaidens' who were then in Zurich and who tried to learn active imagination with the same sanctimonious spirit they tended to bring to their analysis." She has already identified this group as "the doctors Beatrice Hinkle, Kristine Mann, Esther Harding, and Emily Bertine, who often spent their summers in Zurich and were thinking of starting a New York program (the future C. G. Jung Institute)."

Douglas succeeds in contrasting these pioneer Jungians with the sexy and dashing Christiana. As feminist and other revisionists go to work on Jung's long sacrosanct biography (unlike Freud's), it doesn't look like the Jungfrauen, at least for now, are going to make the cut.

More to the point, this book has no use for Harry Murray, the other half of Christiana's Romantic "dyad," or for the elaborate sexual, pornographic, and spiritual schemes that their Jungian-licensed Romanticism invented to celebrate itself: "Harry seemed to have loved joining the drama when he visited Christiana at the Tower," Douglas says, "but he left it up to her to compose it, in much the same way that mistresses, courtesans, and royal favorites have always invented ways to delight and inspire their lord while he contended with the demands of his worldly life."

For Douglas, the woman pays too heavy a price in a Romantic world. "Thus their private world began to take on elements of a Romantic folie-à-deux pretend world, in which Christiana either dedicated herself to his comforts at the Tower or waited alone there for him to return...They did not realize that they were caught by the same regressive emotions that sent troubadours to sing of their desire, Kierkegaard's knight to prefer longing to any communion with a flesh-and-blood woman, or country-and-western singers to croon ballads of ill-fated love...All great Romantic love stories end tragically."

And yet Christiana is so Romantic—she's right up there with Elvis and those other tragic country and western troubadours—that the reader finds it hard to believe this is not what she herself wanted and was in fact best at (I know, she was misled, brainwashed, indoctrinated, had no other options in a male-dominated universe, etc—okay, the theory's possible even if the life can be read in other ways). But was it really so "tragic?" She drowned in the Caribbean, age 70, alcoholic, with Harry near-by, but even this curious episode doesn't quite sound like Greek Tragedy. Ironically, she might herself have said (Romantic to the core) that it was tragic because Harry never did marry her, even after his wife died. Of course, Douglas sees it as tragic in that she betrayed the great chthonic feminine.

"Morgan dove for pearls, while Harry was their connoisseur...Christiana discovered but could not fully decipher, nor did she have the words to convey, a woman's psychological reality...Jung had diverted Morgan away from this task and toward the supposedly more womanly one of inspiring Murray...She tried to adapt herself to an alien task of writing the book about her visions and her life with Murray in the way that he proposed. She thereby betrayed both herself and her visions."

But doesn't one have to respect her judgment, too, somewhere, such as it was, her living as she did, a life which had tremendous moments of ecstasy and grandeur, happiness and pleasure? She wrote:

"Ecstasy—The *It* working through the *me* as instrument—cf. Rilke's perpetual struggle to get *pure* enough & far enough *in* and away from the world enough so this could happen—*Me & my trances.*"

Christiana's own writings have to be constantly repudiated as wrongheaded and misguided in order to argue Douglas's case. Her sadomasochistic diaries are particularly vulnerable to the new feminist puritanism: "My lover is myself explicit. My lover is all my past unconscious power made explicit...Without its passionate ecstasy, craved for as lightening pain. This is the shape my lover has desired. Never will my body know its delicious life without the touch of my lover's strong whip. This is my body that speaks."

And she whips him too: "Mansol knew the rush of lust & asked for the final assertion of the whip. Then Wona struck Mansol with her black whip and it was good to her..."

When it comes to the sadomasochistic part of their fantasies Douglas' comments feel like a wet dishrag of old-fashioned conventional psychoanalytic reductiveness: she reduces their extraordinary fantasy life to childhood problems, a little girl's wish for omnipotence, etc. Her incomprehension of their ecstasies and her anti-Sadean prejudices do not seem at all on Christiana's wavelength. "They possessed," Douglas writes, "all the implements for their experiments—whips, chains, handcuffs, etc.—but there is never a diary entry about physical pain or wounds that needed healing, and both were busily at work the next day. But silence and absence of signs is typical of much family violence and part of its problem." To read what is going on here as "family violence" is just so off-track it's silly. Talk about "sanctimonious spirit!"

"This book traces the conflicting elements in Morgan's character," Douglas writes in the Introduction, "where Romanticism and sadomasochism—its heartless twin—warred together to mute her intensity, stifle her achievements, and veil her legacy." Yet the warring of these forces may have *made* her intensity too. One just doesn't come away from this book feeling that her life was that "wasted" or quite so "stifled." It did, however, become increasingly monotheistic, something it was not when she was meeting with Jung. As she wrote in her Red & Gold Diary, however, a later record of her and Harry's sadomasochistic engagement: "My love is my God and I have no other God but Him...He will drink my blood, devour my flesh, ask for my last sacrifice, take all my spirit, possess me entirely...I give up all my Gods for my *one* God.

Feminists who fault Christiana for "wasting" her visionary explorations of the "chthonic woman" are really faulting her for this monotheistic devotion to Harry. But wouldn't her life have been just as wasted and monolithic had she spent it merely in quest of the monotheistic goddess called "the chthonic woman?" And when we look around at some of our contemporaries who think they have achieved this discovery of the "pure feminine" in the homogenized milk version of Demeter /Persephone/Artemis /Athena/Inanna that is now making the rounds—a little bit of all the ancient goddesses rolled into one and peddled in coffeetable books as The Goddess of the Feminine—who's really being monotheistic?

Morgan's life was as varied as she could stand it, as explorative as she wanted it to be, as man-centered as she insisted. (I'd like to say, "Nobody tied her hands," but Harry, of course, did!) You've got to be a bigger believer in the power of psychoanalysis than I am to say Jung was responsible for all this. Romanticism just isn't about responsibility, and anti-Romantics can't stand it.

To have had Alfred North Whitehead ("Altie" as Christiana called him) popping into your Cambridge apartment for tea because he found you so fascinating, or lingering over breakfast with you in your country house to thrash out ideas, doesn't sound like you're being *too* shortchanged by the inspiratrice life. "During the years of their friendship, Whitehead experienced a new surge of inspiration writing nine books...Among the ones she liked best were *Process and Reality*, *Adventures of Ideas*, and *Nature and Life*, all of which Whitehead discussed with Morgan, cherishing not so much her insights and comments but their power to engender his own." Even if one hates being the inspiratrice to great men, I hope Douglas isn't implying by this that Morgan was even *remotely* capable of writing her own *Process and Reality*.

What a somber utopian burden this important book tries to put on Christiana Morgan, lamenting that she didn't fulfill a 1980s achievement-oriented feminist life (Camille Paglia, for one, seems to have blown that apart in the 90s), instead of celebrating the messy and original, the soulful and explosive one this woman in fact lived.

MORE REVIEWS

Robert Bosnak, *A Little Course in Dreams*. Boston and London: Shambhala, 1993. Pp. 234. $6.00, paper.

This little book (it measures only two inches by three inches) is the best guide to dreamwork we've ever seen. With little chapters on memory exercises to retrieve dreams in the first place, analysis of the dream text, how to listen to what the dream is saying, and how to return to the dream's reality, among others, it will have you waiting impatiently for bedtime to roll around again. The best chapter is the one on alchemy and dreams, a subject that nobody has ever presented as clearly as this:

"When the eye becomes accustomed to the darkness, when the blackness of night has been suffered through, the white light of the moon emerges. The light of the moon is reflected light; it creates a world of imagination that is at home in the dark. The metal is silver. It is a world of echoes, sounds, and voices, helpful voices as well as lunatic convictions and instructions. Reflective surfaces of water, mirrors, laundry, washing machines, soap (the albedo is often called the ablutio, the whitewashing after the nigredo.)"

William G. Doty, *Myths of Masculinity*. New York: Crossroad, 1993. Pp. 243. $24.95, cloth.

From ancient myth to current media image, this is one of the richest and most imaginative of the many new sourcebooks for the Men's Movement:

"Ninety-five percent of men...were dissatisfied with their bodies, and 70 percent felt that they did not come close to their ideal of body type, which was precisely the trim mesomorphic soldier's. Since body type is not largely under voluntary control by dieting or weightlifting...the future portends widespread trouble with male eating and dieting patterns such as are now frequent among women...[P]ectoral and calf implants on males, as well as surgery to produce more shapely buttocks, already accounts for 60 percent of the business at the Beverly Hills Institute of Body Sculpting..."

Henri F. Ellenberger, *Beyond the Unconscious*, ed. Mark S. Micale. Princeton: Princeton University Press, 1993. Pp. 416. $49. 50, cloth.

The author of the magisterial *Discovery of the Unconscious*, unquestionably the most readable book in the historiography of psychology and psychiatry, here presents fourteen further essays, on Freud, Charcot, Janet, Rorschach, Anna O., and others. Particularly engrossing are the essays, "The Concept of 'Maladie Créatrice'" and "The Pathogenic Secret and Its Therapeutics," but readers of *Spring* will be drawn especially to "C. G. Jung and the Story of Helene Preiswerk," written in 1991:

"Today, in retrospect, we are drawn to consider another facet of Carl Gustav's relationship to Helene Preiswerk. At first, it seems that Jung was not much interested in Helene's personality; she was only the subject of an intellectual inquiry. Gradually, in fact, he became bored with her, the more so when he perceived that she was in love with him. The picture he gave of her in his dissertation is one governed by contempt. Later, when he saw her again in Paris...he was attracted to her...Jung went so far as to show to Sabina [Spielrein] an excerpt of his own diary in which he says that he once had a vision of Helly, clad in a luminous white robe...This may well have been the origin of Jung's concept of anima."

Virginia Beane Rutter, *Woman Changing Woman*. San Francisco: HarperSan Francisco, 1993. Pp. 243. $20.00, cloth.

A personal yet professional presentation of woman to woman psychotherapy, this book draws on myths and rituals from the Greeks to the Navajo to illustrate a unique cultural background-and present--for women's work with psyche.

"In long-term psychotherapy and analysis, a woman makes a voluntary decision and commitment to enter therapy. She must be "close-mouthed" about her process at certain times in order to protect the work simmering in the container. She must honor the secrecy of both what she chooses to protect and what is ineffable, or impossible to describe. In performing the ritual of psychotherapy, she undergoes a psychological initiation. By withdrawing behind the "veil" for a time, she dedicates herself to a new state of consciousness. At the end of the ordeal, she has enfolded the experience within, and the veil is lifted."

Marie-Louise von Franz, *Psyche & Matter*. Boston and London: Shambhala, 1992. Pp. 338. $18.00, paper.

Surely no one over the years has written more authoritatively on the over-all subtleties of synchronicity than von Franz. Five of the twelve essays in this collection (the second in a series presenting her work by subject) appear here in English for the first time:

"Although Jung made the only explicit foray of his career into the realm of parapsychology with his proposal of a synchronicity principle, it is precisely a number of parapsychologists who appear to be having difficulties with this new way of thinking. In my opinion, this arises from the fact that many para-psychologists are currently making an intensive effort to achieve acceptability for their field by founding it on a "hard" scientific method, that is, on quanti-tative methods and causal thinking, whereas just what Jung's hypothesis pro-poses is an about-face away from what until now has been considered the only "scientific" way of thinking.

LETTERS TO THE EDITOR

□

Archetypal Psychology Jewish?

To the Editor:

While the title of James Hillman's piece, *How Jewish Is Archetypal Psychology?* [*Spring 53*] is intriguing, it is misleading. The argument seems to be as follows: First there are enduring anti-Semitic models created and maintained by some Christians. Second there are anti-Archetypal Psychology models created and maintained by repressed or unconscious Christians. Third the anti-Archetypal Psychology models appear to be variants of the older anti-Semitic models. Fourth, that this correspondence between the two sets of models suggests the "Jewishness" of Archetypal Psychology.

Here is my problem with this argument: Unless one is to assume that anti-Semitic definitions of Jewishness are accurate portrayals of Jewishness, the fact that Archetypal Psychology can be read to fit those anti-Semitic models says something about the limited ability of Christians to invent new models for its enemies, but nothing about Archetypal Psychology's supposed Jewishness. All one can deduce is that for those unconscious or repressed Christians who still harbor anti-Semitic images and who fear Archetypal Psychology the former can be used to characterize the latter.

On the other hand, I think I understood the underlying message of the piece, namely that Jew-as-outsider corresponds to Archetypal Psychology as outsider. With this I agree. The *ouste-Jude* quality of Archetypal Psychology allows it to sit on the fringes of the normative and to critique it. This is "Jewish" in that it shares with Judaism an aspect of the diasporic Jewish experience, but this historically conditioned outsider status is not innate to Judaism itself.

Ouste-Jude Judaism only applies to Diasporic Judaism. And in fact only to European (Ashkenazi) rather than Oriental (Sephardic) Jewish experience—all the more curious seeing as how this essay was written to commemorate the expulsion of the Jews from Spain in 1492. Jews were expelled from Spain not because they were outsiders, but because they had become too powerful as insiders. The expulsion was a power play designed to capture Jewish wealth. That is why it had to be followed up by the Inquisition. Too many wealthy and powerful Jews converted to Catholicism, kept their wealth intact and continued to threaten the crown and the church with a budding independent and international financial empire.

To test the article's theory further, one would have to see how it applies in modern day Israel. Here Judaism is the status-quo. Here Archetypal Psychology's deconstructionism would be a Goyish intrusion, not a Jewish one. Do Israeli Jewish psychologists seeking to resurrect the inner child see Archetypal Psychology as child-killing? Do these Jews use Christian anti-Semitic models in their attacks on Archetypal Psychology? It would be interesting to find out.

Do I find the article to be entirely wrong-headed? Not at all. In fact, I found it most insightful and accurate, and, when I had finished reading it for the second time, I found myself wishing that the Judaism it describes was in fact the Judaism I know. The elements are there, but...

Judaism as god slayer: Yes! Look at the folk tales surrounding Abraham who destroyed the idols that were his family's livelihood. Look at Genesis' passionate attacks on paganism and polytheism. Now if we could only slay YHVH and encounter the Is behind the Ism! But alas, no.

Judaism as the imageless: Yes! Thou shalt have no gods beside Me (defining Me at the Burning Bush as infinite Being). A Judaism without graven images, faithful to the faceless One behind the masked Many. But instead we have made a god of tradition and a tradition of God.

Jew as wanderer: Yes! Playing the bee to humanity's flower bridging civilizations and affecting dialogue and synthesis. Judaism was born and nurtured at the crossroads of the world's civilizations. Our creativity was in response to the multiculturalism that was our historical experience. But what do we have today? We are a nation like any other, and the Judaism of Israel is spiritually moribund and morally bankrupt.

Jew as doubter: I only wish this were true. Jews are passionate believers: that is why we have given the world Christianity, Marxism, Freudianism, Secularism, Zionism. Jews believe too much. Doubt is the great liberator. And doubting even doubt the greater freedom. Both orthodox and liberal Jews fail to question, fail to doubt.

Judaism as Tikkun ha-Olam/world repair: This is true. Jesus chastised the Jews saying, "What matters is what comes out of one's mouth not what goes into it." Judaism disagrees. Judaism teaches that we are what we eat emotionally, politically, physically, sexually, spiritually, intellectually, etc. Jews have not abandoned the mission of Judaism to repair the world with justice (which is why we find so many Jews in the forefront of social justice issues and movements), we simply no longer find Judaism relevant to that mission.

I have been a student of both Hillman and Jung for many years. I have always felt the innate "Jewishness" of Archetypal Psychology, though my understanding of both is carefully defined to allow such a confluence.

I imagine that my comments are in a sense nitpicking. But nitpicking is the essence of *pilpul*, talmudic inquiry. And, as the article so wonderfully puts it: "Jews don't grow, they study."

Rabbi Rami M. Shapiro
Temple Beth Or
Miami, Florida

◻

Asher's Communitarian Self

To the Editor:

One does not have to be a "hardcore, diehard" Jungian (thus the Editors of *Spring 54*) to have difficulties with the views expressed in Charles Asher's article, "The Communitarian Self as (God) Ultimate Reality." I have no stake in Jung's self concept and only recently distanced myself publicly from it in my book *Animus Psychologie* as I have many times before, so it is not natural for me to come to its defense. But not only my respect for Jung and for the psychological reality he was wrestling with makes me do just that. I also feel the need to reply because Asher's paper seems to express a reversal of essential tenets and concerns of Archetypal Psychology (or what it once used to be), even while pretending to be an exponent of Archetypal Psychology.

Asher charges that Jung's self concept is under the spell of Zwingli's theistic image of God as all-powerful will requiring a defeated and cowering ego and is expressive of a "collision theology" with its "power obsession" ("ego-self power dynamics"). He rejects it because according to him it is "outmoded," "woefully inadequate" and "has tragic consequences." It leaves the "future of Jungian thought and practice in serious jeopardy...The theological foundations of Jung's self concept are sick unto death." And so he wants to "re-form psychological thought and especially Jung's self concept."

Asher models his "Jungian self re-formation" after *the* Reformation, explicitly stylizing his theses according to Luther's 95 theses and ending with his version of Luther's "Here I stand." The word "reformation" can mean different things. For the Reformation itself it meant a fundamental deepening of doctrine, the radicalization of its understanding, and a return (seeing through) to its origins by so-to-speak burning away *"omnes superfluitates"*—in other words a kind of *destillatio, sublimatio, mundificatio.* Asher, in purposely numbering his 10 sections as 9.5 theses (theses 1-9 plus thesis #9.5) to bring them in some sort of numerical comparability with Luther's 95 theses, seems to want us to understand that his re-formation has another meaning: that of a *reduction* to only 10% of the depth and weight of traditional Jungian thought. And indeed, when he criticizes Jung's self concept, he does not first re-create a sense of the momentous psychological issue Jung was struggling with in his self psychology. He does not raise us to a level where we could hope to reach into the dimension where the full and living reality Jung tried to capture under the name of "self" is located. No, he brings the self concept down to the status that his own concepts have, that of mere "imaginings," of abstract constructs. Thus he attacks only the sapless, formalistic definitions of "self," in other words, his own abstractions, or a castrated self, not the real experience or the experienced reality that the self was for Jung. A real critique of the "self" (which is legitimate, even needed) would have to address the Jungian self in its highest determination, in its fullest and most powerful sense and where it is at its best, i.e., where it is most richly loaded with soul substance. It would have to show why it does not do justice to the reality that it attempts to express.

This discount, or better, clearance sale approach to traditional (Jungian and theological) thought is revealed most painfully in how Asher reacts to the question of Trinity and to the Book of Job. What hurts here is the loss of soul. His answer to theology's and Jung's struggles with the problem of Trinity is a flippant, "Following process thought I suggest we stop numbering!" (p. 83). As if the Three that are One and Jung's attempt to add a Fourth to the Three were nothing but a numbering game just like Asher's own trifling with the 95 theses.

There is a total insensitivity to the soul dimension of the trinity theme, to the depth and weight the soul has invested into it by involving, over centuries, some of the greatest minds and deepest souls of the Christian West along with their suffering as well as with their bliss in it. The psychological reality at stake here is simply not seen. With a similar flippancy Asher can reduce the problem of Job to a *quantité negligeable*.

Asher's theses are about "(God) Ultimate Reality" or "Ultimate Reality (God)." Here God is bracketed, relegated to a secondary status. Archetypal psychology's "Personifying" is out, abstract concepts are in. The parentheses around God are the visual expression of the attempt to do God in: to deprive him of his autonomy and wildness by imprisoning him safely in his brackets. God is to be domesticated. Whereas the word "God" has some of the quality of a proper name by which a reality or living subject is *evoked* (potentially projecting as a real Other into our human sphere and threatening us with some claim), "Ultimate Reality" is a concept of our making (that at best signifies, or refers to, a real object). With such a concept we stay on this side of our subjectivity and humanness. We are using a term that is completely at our disposal, because it stems solely from our "imaginings." We stay among ourselves, humans among humans, completely free to indulge in our fantasies *about* its real or imagined referent. Archetypal psychology's "Dehumanizing" is canceled.

The taming of God does not only occur visually by means of punctuation marks but also linguistically (or stylistically). Where once people would have said, e.g., "The fear of the Lord is the beginning of wisdom" as well as "I will fear no evil, for thou art with me," we now hear that the "*image* of a God/self as responsive love seems to dispel my fears of the classical theological and Jungian self *concept image*" (p. 94, my emphasis). One image dispels the fear of another image, a self-contained game between images. Reality or a *real* God is held at bay, even made redundant. As far as I am concerned, I might come to fear something real, the Lord or the world, the events of life, but how to fear a concept image *of* God I must still learn. And I doubt whether my *imagings* of God as responsive love would dispel my real fears if I were, e.g., in a concentration camp or in situations like Bosnia, Angola, Somalia. For Asher, "it is this process God/self *imagining* that supports my consciousness of them in clinical practice and daily life" (p. 94, my emphasis), just as "Power is exercised by a God/self *imagining* who ..." (p. 93, my emphasis) and not, as one would expect, by God himself. Asher linguistically immunizes himself from reality or from God as a reality by interposing between himself and God the words image and imaginings, depotentiating God by encapsulating him in them as their mere object or content. God, prior to being the subject of sentences elaborating what he is or does is appropriated by the ego and subjugated to its own fantasies.

Beyond what punctuation and formulations betray, this depotentiation is also the thrust of his thematic argument, which is a continued attack on the "classical theistic tension, at the core of Jung's self/ego concept" (p. 90) and tries to get rid of the ideas of God as powerful will, of the encounter or conflict between God's will and my own will, of the ego's having to die, of shadow and Evil as inherent in God. Of course, all these ideas are indeed up for debate. But Asher never really enters into a debate, never seriously delves into these ideas trying to see through to their archetypal depth or demonstrating their inherent weakness and contradictions, but rather contents himself with sweeping assertions about their obsoleteness as well as their danger for therapy and life, sometimes giving obviously distorting interpretations of them: with the Zwinglian-Jungian emphasis on God's all-powerful will, humans and the ego "are left passive; the world is left dead and unimportant," p. 90. Were Zwingli and Jung passive, the world for them dead and unimportant? Did Jung have and aim for a cowering ego? Asher maintains that Jung's self-concept, "of course, immediately undervalues the world of ego consciousness as a secondary development" (p. 84)—as if in the early days of Archetypal Psychology Jung had never been criticized for the opposite, for his over-valuation of the ego. In thesis 6 Asher presents Jung's thought as stressing abstract totality and the universal, whereas with his, Asher's, "radically different starting point...the focus is on the particular...The concrete is given priority over the abstract..."—as if Jung's emphasis had not been on the concrete. On the contrary, I have doubts whether Asher's alleged emphasis on the concrete is truly concrete and not much rather abstract in a hidden way: one might consult here Hegel's little piece on "Who thinks abstractly?"

Instead of entering into a debate on Jung's position, Asher merely "rejects" it and offers "alternative imaginings" in its place. This wholesale rejection together with the establishment of alternatives I take to indicate that Asher does not primarily reject these theses on intellectual grounds, but because of ideological needs, so that an "ideology-critique" is in place. The attack on the theistic ideas of God seems to be in the service of a worldview and a view (not really of God, but) of "Ultimate Reality" (whatever that may mean) that are supposed to "metaphysically" authorize a particular middle-class "postmodern" lifestyle and to protect this life-style from being disturbed or threatened by an encounter with reality as a real Other (the real world or a real God). It is the ideology of a consciousness that wants to stay unassailably enwrapped in its own imaginings and therefore, not for legitimate philosophical, theological, or psychological reasons, needs to do away with the idea of a possibly overwhelming God that might mean the defeat of such an ego. The mere idea of man "utterly abandoned to God" (Jung) or of the defeat of the ego is "nauseating" to this consciousness (cf. p. 88). If this is the Archetypal Psychology of the Nineties, Archetypal Psychology has come round full circle. It began, among other things, as an attack on ego-psychology and with the idea of a "one-way movement" out of the ego's morning traffic into the dark, toward the underworld, to paraphrase Hillman, *The Dream and the Underworld*, p. 1. Now, the goal is an *"enhancement* of the ego" (p. 74). The sense of the dignity and psychological legitimacy of a truly religious existence (in contrast to the "mundane" life in the spirit of the ego) is lost.

When the allegedly "needless oppositionalism...between creator and creature" (p. 84) is rejected, I suspect that this is also in the service of an ego world enclosed in itself without Other. This is not to say that on the basis of serious philosophical or psycho-theological reason one might not come to a similar conclusion. But the lack of such reasons in this paper and its whole thrust support my suspicion. For Asher, the Jungian self or God *must not* be transcendent. God must be eliminated as autonomous vis-à-vis and be pulled into ego-consciousness, so that the repressed returns as an ego-syntonic content or object within consciousness. Everything is submerged in one great whole of absolute relatedness, one great process, everything affecting everything else, but there is no real Other. God is just "an occasion among other occasions" (p. 86) within this "cosmic" whole devoid of alterity. Correspondingly, Evil, shadow, tragedy and true suffering (like Job's) have no real place here. Archetypal Psychology's "Pathologizing as a soul-making" is a thing of the past. God is (more or less) only good, supremely responsive love, and "Evil is transformed into novel possibilities for each moment of becoming" (p. 89), creating "ever new possibilities" (p. 90); "The all-inclusive well-being of the many in community is the reflection of God's image in the world" (p. 77, Asher quoting M. Suchocki). All this will certainly be Good News for the Bosnian Moslems.

One has to keep in mind that these ideas were written down at a time when all over the world there are civil wars, mass murders, ethnic cleansings, racial tensions, nations falling apart, the consensus of societies splitting up into radical, often fanatic fractions, the communal sense dwindling in favor of an egotistical self- or group-interest, in order to realize how much this thinking is cut off from reality. Communal spirit, relatedness, supreme openness for everything novel, supremely responsive love, the all-inclusive well-being of the many in community—these are all honorable and beautiful ideals. There is nothing to be said against them. But are they real? Even *Ultimate* Reality? They are utopian.

But precisely because they are utopian, they have to be *called* Ultimate Reality. This designation is, first, the claim to realness, which is, secondly, blown up to ultimate reality, that in turn is deified by way of capitalization. The Romans said, "*lucus a non lucendo.*" So here we can say, this imagining has to use the name ultimate reality, nay Ultimate Reality, because this utopia is not real of its own accord. This is the dialectic of inflation (in the monetary, not the Jungian sense); more and more money is printed, more and more zeroes are added to the numbers on it, so that everyone is a millionaire—only, for his million he can at best buy a loaf of bread. The millions are worthless; the millionaire is just as poor as before. What the utopia lacks in the way of solidarity, it gains in linguistic pompousness.

"Ultimate Reality" implies some counterpart, a preliminary or peripheral reality, much like in Kant the Thing-in-itself has the Appearance, and in Plato the nouminal (the realm of Forms) has the phenomenal as its counterpart. But whereas for Plato it was the task of the philosopher to ascend from the "Cave" to the realm of Forms so as to come into a cognitive relation with reality, with truth, there is no such move in Asher's thinking. Asher has eliminated all real otherness. He has comfortably settled in the Cave and is enclosed in *his own* "imaginings" *about* an Ultimate Reality, about relatedness, responsive love etc., i.e., with watching the shades on the wall of his Cave. What you get in the Cave is not "Dreams of a Spirit-Seer" but something similar: imaginings of an Ultimate-Reality-seer.

This is again a point where Archetypal Psychology is reversed. Henry Corbin coined the term imaginal in contradistinction to the imaginary, to our imaginings. He spoke of the *imaginatio vera*, of that kind of imagination that is cognitive, poetic as opposed to utopian fantasies, to the figments of the mind. Cognition is not inherent in Asher's imaginings. They are self-sufficient. They need no outside referent. And the specific purpose of the particular imaginings he offers in this article is to advocate and authorize the idea of an imagining without referent and to eliminate the idea of any thought of a truth that could be known. When asked about God Jung did not say, I imagine God, but, I know of God. And his psychology is an attempt to formulate psychological reality, not to present "alternative imaginings" as if he were an author of children's stories. He claimed that he was a scientist, which makes sense at least inasmuch as he was indeed in search of truth.

Asher presents as one of his alternative imaginings the idea of God as concrete, definite, particular and incarnated. But this is only what he says. His behavior is different. When he comes up against an idea of a truly concrete, particular God (Jung's God in the tradition of the Reformation) he rejects it. Precisely because Jung's God was not a philosophical universal, not an abstraction, but was, as psychologically real, a concrete historical and cultural given, Jung had to live with the "Zwinglian" God. He could not escape from his real tradition to any alternative. Jung didn't have a choice, nor other options. His God was local, definite. Jung had to take his prima materia as he found it, with the whole weight of history and all the painful, perhaps even tragic complexities that it came with. He had to start from where the soul actually happened to be. He was not free to imagine a "better" God that might have been more to his liking, not a do-it-yourself God. But this is the very reason why Asher rejects it: as definite, this God is limiting, nailing us down in our real tradition. Asher does not demonstrate that (and how) Jung's God is outdated. But he involuntarily shows that what motivates him is the wish to avoid the relentless realness of God. He wants to be free. He wants alternatives. He has shaken off the weight of history. His "(God)" is not embedded in any tradition; it is

his own* free-floating imagination and deserves to be put into parentheses or to be renamed into the abstract-universal concept "Ultimate
Reality." And it *can* be a free-floating imagination because it is safely
confined in its brackets. Asher attacks the idea of the creation *ex nihilo*,
but he does not seem to realize that this is the very archetypal image *he*
is sitting in. For he is absolutely free to imagine his alternatives. He is
the architect or designer of his Ultimate Reality imaginings (he is the
designer psychologically, even if factually he may rely on other
authors for some of his ideas). No prima materia that he would be
stuck with, no real, local tradition that would bind him. If he is not
happy with one view, such as with Jung's Protestant heritage, he just
pushes the button on his remote control to turn it off ("reject it") and
to tune into another station: an alternative imagining after his own liking.

I spoke of Asher's view as an ideology. The previous sentence allows
me to be more specific. It is the ideology logically defined by the institution of television. It is the faith (far removed from Robert Grinnell's
"psychological faith") of a humankind that is ready to cocoon itself in
cyberspace, ready to voluntarily descend into the Platonic Cave, in order to comfortably watch the images on its back wall. People know-
ingly chaining themselves so that they are fixed in a position with their
backs to reality and to any real God outside the Cave.

And Asher's Ultimate Reality? This notion does not add anything
substantial to that of peripheral reality. It is different only in that it is
the *glorified* peripheral, arbitrarily furnished with the highest possible
rank, that of absoluteness. E.g., it is the "political 'team image'" of Bill
and Hillary Clinton and the Gores "raised to ultimacy" (p. 76).
"Ultimate Reality" only duplicates the flat image of everyday reality,
but while doing so inflates this clone with a higher emotional value,
with an air of grandeur. Psychologically seen through, it is nothing
more than the reification and deification of Asher's methodological
point-of-view, the unreflected projection forward onto the Cave's wall

---

*"His own" is not supposed to suggest that Asher is all alone with his view.
There are others who have similar convictions and Asher refers to some such
authors. What is suggested is that in each case where these convictions are held
they are each author's own in the sense of "cut off from tradition" and
"subjective."

of the interests unconsciously guiding the "Last Man" (Nietzsche) from behind. Ontologically speaking, Ultimate Reality is a euphemistic and idolizing name for the opposite of reality, for "*virtual reality*," whose only *real, but unacknowledged and hidden God* ("deus absconditus") is Money, Big Capital.

Roberts Avens said, "Imagination *is* reality." If we learn our lesson from Asher, we have to say, "Alternative imaginings *are* Ultimate Reality, and Ultimate Reality *is* Cyberspace." Every TV-viewer *is* ipso facto an Ultimate Reality-seer.

The communitarian self is, logically speaking, the self of all the people equally "chained" to their TV armchairs. And what is communitarian about it is the fact that all are united not necessarily in viewing the same program, but in viewing in the same mode; whatever they are watching they view it *as* "television show." It is the nature of the TV presentation that in it all reality returns as the repressed in the comfort of the Cave called "living room." But it returns only in the form of images *of* reality, i.e. in the form of a bracketed "(reality)," a bracketed "(God)." And the comfort expressing itself in the ideas of Ultimate Reality as communitarian, as universal relatedness, as supremely responsive love results from the knowledge that one is living in the Cave and that it serves as our psychological or logical (not physical) air-raid shelter. This shelter's power to shelter is due to the fact that in it one comes in touch with reality only as imagined reality or TV image, while reality in its pressing, possibly overwhelming, perhaps even ego-defeating realness, be it brutal or blissful, is once and for all, namely *logically*, banished to the realm outside the Cave, behind our backs, to the real (but disowned) Bosnia, the real (but disowned) slums, our real (but disowned) personal lives.

A psychotherapy informed by this idea of a communitarian self must have the overall purpose of ritually transporting our existence from real life into the Cave, turning us into (logical, not literal) Cave dwellers, into (logical) troglodytes; it must have the purpose of logically translating reality into the status of virtuality, the status so-to-speak of shades appearing on that "Cave wall" that in the physical realm we call TV set and in the psychological realm "our imagination."

Asher ends his article with his credo, for which he adapts a saying by Luther. "Here I stand before these reflections. Tomorrow I can do other—as these imaginings process into another moment of becoming." The first sentence is contradicted by the second. He who speaks thus doesn't know what standing means. He is not taking a stand at all. Luther, when he was (allegedly) speaking his "Here I stand," knew that he was staking his life. He did not relate his "imaginings," imaginings that may come and go like moods, but he spoke with the claim of speaking the truth. And this is why he was truly standing, had a real "standpoint." But Asher is just speaking for the moment. Even more: while speaking today, Asher already anticipates tomorrow's supersession of his present imaginings, himself undermining any claim to validity or truth they might come with. He does not stand by his own conviction. Rather than standing, he is riding the waves, ready to be moved by the next mood, image, or fad. If this is his attitude, why does he *write*? Why does he want his writing to be in *print*? Writing and printing presuppose an idea of "eternity" or at least lasting duration. Strictly speaking, according to his own "process thought" (as far as it goes), he could neither write, nor speak. He could only utter momentary *exclamations*— or "talk" (talk as in "talk-show").

His is the kind of standing that mirrors that of our politicians when they solemnly declare with respect to former Yugoslavia that they will never accept border changes brought about by military means or ethnic cleansing. The retraction is built into the "position" taken.

Heraclitus, whom Asher imagines to be one of his authorities for his "process thought," deposited his book in the temple of Artemis. This shows his own esteem for it. It was definitely not conceived for the moment, but for "eternity." Asher by contrast declares his own reflections to be a priori disposable, recyclable. Should this be where *Spring* is heading? A journal not only printed on 100% recycled paper, but also printing articles a priori conceived as 100% recyclable? Today it seems to be dawning on society's consciousness that manufacturers will have to be obligated, *prior* to manufacturing their products, to develop a concrete concept of how to dispose of or recycle them. This brings out the hitherto hidden truth about industrial products, about all the beautiful commodities that we consumers buy: *logically* they are trash to begin with, a priori, and not only once they have become unusable. They are produced *as trash*. Could it be that the "process thought" hailed by Asher is the acted out glorification of the hidden metaphysics of a throw-away society? And that the agnosticism and indifferentism inherent in this process thought as well as in this free-floating imagining is the counterpart or other side of (and therefore the *same* as) the fanatic fundamentalism we experience today? They are both two forms of the expression of modern man's existence in the Cave. The one rejoices over the ever novel possibilities made available by the constant flux of shows in one channel, and by being able to switch from one channel to another, and it substitutes the multitude of momentary images for truth, reality, necessity, and God; the other (equally far removed from the reality outside the Cave) pretends to rescue the sense of reality and God by subjectively demanding for one single show or imagining the status of absolute truth and therefore total obedience, and it blinds itself to the mere show character of its show and the arbitrariness of its demands.

Would it not be the task of a *real* psychology to resist these two opposite defenses and to hold its place between them? Would it not be its task to simply see through to the locus of our so-called "postmodern" existence (the Cave) and, by bringing this insight to consciousness, connect the soul—of course not with reality itself outside the Cave (which would merely be the defensive attempt to undo the postmodern soul's move into the Cave), but with the soul's *loss* of reality, of soul, of God? A loss that was inflicted upon the soul by no other than the soul itself. A loss that wants to be consciously *felt* (not corrected, not repaired—but not glorified and raised to the status of a religion either).

Wolfgang Giegerich
Stuttgart, Germany

◻

Ultimate Reality Is Not God

To the Editor:

Charles Asher's article, "The Communitarian Self as (God) Ultimate Reality" in *Spring 54* seems to indicate that we—in our communicative being—are, in fact, the being of God. This is going some steps beyond A. N. Whitehead, and perhaps some steps even beyond David Ray Griffin (whose influence shows so strongly on every page). It is an intriguing notion, traceable at least to Durkheim. Theses 1 to 5 seem to follow from this and open the way for vast imaginings. In theses 6 & 7, however, a good archetypal polytheist can feel a theological rationalist purge beginning. With Asher's denial of Jung's ego/self either/or dynamism, it is surprising to read him doing *either/or* as *Jung/Whitehead*. Such dichotomism is patently unfair to Jung (though not necessarily to Jungian therapists) since Jung indicated ego must always be retained not as unconscious personality but as *persona* through which we enter the stage of the world. Furthermore, the metaphoric similarities between Jung and Whitehead are extensive, I think, and could only seem exclusive to logical positivists or to committed theocentrists like D. R. Griffin and Charles Asher.

Asher's utilitarian approach claims to choose a cosmology which "works" best in psychotherapy. He seems to recognize the importance of transformation with his "Behold the new!" but then, with theses 8, 9, & 9.5, he narrows the walk of the Sacred Way by being determinative about the ends, the goals, or the aims of that transformation. God and goodness—and what next, productivity?—are good aims, no doubt. But it seems to me that Whitehead's *eternal objects* better symbolize those potentials or ideals that teleologically *inspire* action to give them form, however imperfect.

These eternal objects, as has been noted, are reminiscent of Platonic ideal forms, Jungian archetypes and archetypal gods. The advantage of such a polytheistic cosmology is that our ideal aims are not limited by our limited notions of good and evil and God (Ultimate Reality) is not similarly delimited. (Besides, a cosmos in which God furthers only "good" creativity and determines that "bad" creativity actually un-creates could never move into experimental novelty—could never, in fact, get started since good creativity would be immediately undone by bad.) Finally, such eternal objects (archetypes) are no doubt supremely responsive to love (as Asher feels God to be) but in some cases this love may be returned as possession, as in mania or obsession. These are the dangers of a polytheistic cosmos which contains good, evil, and all the tricksterisms in between. Ultimate reality here is not God—whether communitarian or process—but the elision among eternally penultimate archetypal images.

Greg Nixon
Baton Rouge, Louisiana

☐

Cynical Obfusations

To the Editor:

Goodness! You see it not? The increasing, critical intellectualism that rends and splits and disparages with cynical obfuscations and caustic put-downs? The descendants and inheritors of Jung's legacy must needs destroy, much as Cronos destroyed Saturn, Zeus destroyed Cronos; without the intervening lessons of Christian or Buddhist charity and loving kindness. Put another way: it's Fraser's King of the Wood syndrome all over again: "Who gets to knock off the king in order to be king." The transcendent function is passé if not forgotten. How Jung's children have fallen! The shadow in ascendency. Doesn't anybody ever learn? Before I continue, I better define, so you know where I'm coming from:

A. Definitions.
   1. "Caustic": Severely critical or sarcastic.
   2. "Cynical":
      a. Distrusting or disparaging the motives of others;
      b. Showing contempt for accepted standards of honesty or morality of others ... esp. by actions that exploit the scruples of others. (*Random House Dictionary of the English Language*)

A. Specific examples: *Spring 54.*

Giegerich: "The soul first made itself through killing. It killed itself into being." (The German psyche is alive and well, despite two World Wars!) "Soul and consciousness are not natural." Implied: a child has no soul, hence the child is "natural?" Implied: when hoods kill they gain a soul? Implied: the Jews were sacrificed by the millions to bolster the soul of the German collective? The soul of the child, we once were told, is innocent. To achieve soul adulthood, we must then collectively kill— make human sacrifice, literally if not psychologically. The transcendent function of Jesus was supposed to have made this passé. By the way, please define soul.

Miller: "'...Have a nice day' is a wish for a day that we all know damned well no real day in our world can be." No chance of Maslow's peak experience in this: i.e. Pierre in Tolstoy's *War & Peace*—but that's only fiction—or Victor Frankel's experience. This reveals more of the author's psyche than it displays empirical truth.

Hartman: "I believe typology was simply (note the reductionism) the vehicle that Jung chose to come to grips with the problem of psychic energy..." The entire article cynically disparages typology, even selectively and conveniently using Jung's own words, completely disregarding the heuristic implications explicit and implicit in the larger body of Jung's writings on typology. This also reveals more of the author's psyche than displaying empirical truth. (More on this below.)

Note: This isn't the only article you've run recently wherein Jung's typology is disparaged. Analysts don't want to be analysed, do they?

Asher: Regarding a *Communitarian Godhead*: Granted, the author's thesis has some validity. But: in disparaging "Jungian psychology and much post-Jungian thought...subtly perpetuated by Jung's self-concept" he adds: "How frantically we cling to them hoping to mitigate Jung's indescrete turd dropping God...The theological foundations of Jung's self-concept are sick unto death. I would hasten their death." Paraphrased: It's not Jung's way; it's MY WAY. The King of the Wood (or King of the Shitpile) syndrome. A colossal ego trip. The entire article, to my mind, is a caustic and cynical putdown. Aside from that, the author has the audacious effrontery to speak for God. Somewhere Jung said (I'm paraphrasing) that all statements made concerning God are meaningless: they cannot be proven or disproven, for they deal with totality. That statement, in itself, tends to destroy the author's entire premise.

Hillman: Regarding *Alchemical Blue*: This is so intellectually obfuscating that the author loses all touch with "the spirit." My God: I'm an artist and taught art history, and I'll be damned if I understand what the hell he is really saying. This article is only for adepts initiated into the sanctum sanctorum of Hillman's differentiated thinking function. The implied cynicism of the author's attitude towards those of us operating with other functions dominant is obvious.

General examples.

Hillman: *How Jewish is Archetypal Psychology? (Just a Little Note.)* The entire article is caustic. (Its validity is not in question.) The subtitle is a caustic keynote. (*Spring 53*)

Caldwell: *Piety and Reaction in C. S. Lewis.* The entire article is a cynical, disparaging and sarcastic putdown. (And I'm not a particular fan of

C. S. Lewis—except for his science fiction trilogy—and indeed, the ending of *Perelandra* was a bit too much. On the other hand, *That Hideous Strength* accurately pictures the industrial-ecological disaster towards which we are headed. And what's so "pious" about that?) Aside from the author's caustic disparagement of Lewis' "horrible" wartime experience—it's obvious he's never experienced wartime horror, otherwise he wouldn't be so cavalier about it and have more empathy towards one who did—it's just too difficult and horrible to talk about—his view of Joy Davidman as "a predatory American litterateuse," without justifying this reductionist judgment, is the height of cynicism. In what way would a terminally ill woman be predatory? (*Spring 52*)

A thought: Why don't you guys tackle the piety of the son-of-a bitch TV evangalists, or the piety of the murderous pro-lifers, or the self-righteous and arrogant piety of the celibate priesthood instead of pussy-footing around as you did in the article *The Dominant/Submissive*—and the entire issue, for that matter? Such would be a hell of a lot more relevant than attacking the questionable, yet perhaps honest, and long dead, piety of C. S. Lewis.

Hillman: *Recovery*: Here, I feel, sarcasm is holy justified, especially the first paragraph on p. 123. The more communicative self of Hillman is allowed expression. He should go for more of this, so we peons can better understand him. (*Spring 52*) Yet, overall:

Hillman: *We've had a hundred years of psychotherapy and the world's getting worse* is heavy into cynicism. Maybe I'm wrong here. Maybe I should substitute the word pessimistic.

C. General, implicit examples.

1. There seems to be an increasing, overarching sarcastic cutting and putting down of Jung and his work for the sake of elevating the individual authors' analytical selves (self-inflation case).

2. I also feel there is increasing one-upsmanship in dealing with the pros and cons of analytical theory—one good-old-boy clique pitted against another such. In this case it is also, it seems to me, predicated on self-inflation rather than on a search for truth.

3. Finally, and in particular, there seems to be a disparagement and denigration of Jung's typology, with no impartial examination into the positive effects and heuristic possibilities of this theory. And indeed, if I have read it right, Jung regarded his typology theory as primarily

heuristic, which no one seems to consider anymore. (Incidentally, my master's thesis, which, according to the dean of graduate studies, was the equivalent of two doctorates, was on the influence of an individual's typology which determines the production-appreciation of art. And that was a long time ago.)

D. In sum—and you didn't ask me for this so I'm giving it gratuitously—there seems to be a decided over-intellectualizing trend in the descendents of Jung for the sake of the personal ego and at the expense of the transcendent function. Obviously, there are further examples, but I haven't the time nor do I desire to try your patience. I wouldn't go to any of these cats for analysis—I'd shun them like the plague; and I've had 11 years of so-called individuation!

I'm finished. Now I can continue to prepare for our vacation. My wife and I are going down the Colorado River through the Grand Canyon on a two week dory trip. We did it two years ago and found it so overwhelming, spiritually, that we have to go back to see what we missed. Maybe more of your analyst-writers should do this—it would tend to compensate for their intellectual hubris. And despite my comments, I do enjoy your publication. It keeps opening my eyes further, willy-nilly, to both the positive and negative.

Sincerely,
A. Walter
Madera, California

P.S. Suggest you look into the publications of the Institute of Noetic Sciences whose prime philosophical function is to increase human consciousness in all areas; something, it seems, analytical psychologists have forgotten.

New M.A. Program in Mythological Studies

Pacifica has added Mythological Studies to its respected Graduate programs in Depth Psychology

Pacifica Graduate Institute introduces a unique Masters degree program in Mythological Studies that explores worldwide sacred traditions, symbolism, and ritual in light of the concepts of archetypal and depth psychology.

The content of this two-year program is appropriate for adult students who are writers, artists, educators, religious leaders, managers, and others who wish to integrate mythological themes in their creative careers. This degree is preparatory to a Ph.D. program.

Classes begin in Fall 1994 and will be held in a monthly three-day retreat format, Mondays–Wednesdays.

PSYCHOLOGY PROGRAMS

Pacifica also offers a Ph.D. in Clinical Psychology and an M.A. in Counseling Psychology. Students who journey from all points in the country to participate in these degree programs are in residence on the campus when classes meet each month over a three-day weekend.

ARCHIVES AND LIBRARY

The Joseph Campbell Archives, which houses the personal library and papers of the late mythologist, and the special psychological holdings of the Institute's Graduate Research Library provide a unique combination of resources for students and visiting scholars.

VISITING SCHOLARS

The new Mythological Studies program continues Pacifica's innovative tradition of interdisciplinary curriculum highlighted each quarter by noted guest speakers. Recent visiting scholars have included Christine Downing, Elinor Gadon, Marija Gimbutas, James Hillman, David Miller, and Marion Woodman.

PACIFICA
GRADUATE INSTITUTE
Site of The Joseph Campbell Archives and Library

**249 Lambert Road
Carpinteria, California 93013**
(805) 969-3626
Fax (805) 565-1932

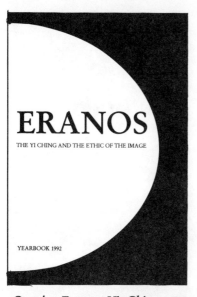

Honoring the Mysteries of Love and Relationship

SOUL MATES
Thomas Moore

As Thomas Moore pointed out in *Care of the Soul*, the soul thrives under certain conditions, especially intimacy, attachment and involvement. In *Soul Mates* Moore shows how the need to love and to connect with others leads inevitably not only into intimacy but also into many

kinds of difficulty and even failure. But the book emphasizes that if we are willing to live through these difficulties, life is enriched and the soul thrives. 320 pages; hardcover; ISBN 0-06-016928-1; $25.00

CARE OF THE SOUL
A Guide for Cultivating Depth and Sacredness in Everyday Life

In this bestseller, now available in paperback, Thomas Moore offers a completely new way of thinking about daily life and proposes a therapeutic lifestyle that focuses on looking more deeply into emotional problems and sensing sacredness in ordinary things.
336 pages; paperback; ISBN 0-06-092224-9; $12.00

Available in Bookstores in January
HarperCollins*Publishers*

CIIS

A graduate school where intellect, intuition and the ageless wisdom of diverse cultures converge.

Integrating Eastern and Western knowledge, the California Institute of Integral Studies is an accredited graduate school with innovative programs leading to M.A. and Ph.D. degrees in:

Business
Clinical Psychology
Drama Therapy
East-West Psychology
Integral Counseling Psychology
Integral Health Studies
Integral Studies
Organizational Development & Transformation
Philosophy & Religion
Social & Cultural Anthropology
Somatics

Also offering a
BA Completion Program

Introducing studies in
Expressive Arts Therapy
Women's Spirituality

V.A. approved. Federal loans and scholarships available to qualified students. A number of foreign and minority scholarships are available annually. Auditors welcome.

California Institute of Integral Studies

For information write :
Box SP, 765 Ashbury Street, San Francisco CA 94117
(415) 753-6100

William Bramhall

Earn the degree of your dreams.

The Program in Psychoanalytic Studies—an inclusive and interdisciplinary master's program—emphasizes the study of psychoanalysis from a social science perspective in a humanities context. Particular attention is paid to both Social and Political Thought and Gender Studies. Students analyze Freudians—From Freud to Jacques Lacan and Beyond; and Jungians— From Jung to James Hillman and Beyond.

Call toll-free 1-800-523-5411 (in NYC 212-229-5710) for a detailed fact sheet describing admission to this master's degree program. Or write: New School for Social Research, The Graduate Faculty, Admissions Office, 65 Fifth Ave., New York, N.Y. 10003.

Master's Degree in Psychoanalytic Studies
New School for Social Research

THE SOUNDINGS
CROSSWORD

For *Soundings* readers who want their answers in black and white.

TIME: 20 min, pre-Cartesian; 15 min, post-Kantian; 10 min, post-modern, 5 min, genius; 1 min, apostle

DOWN:

1. The Prodigal got one, but his brother didn't
2. As Keats saw it, a fair attitude
3. Egyptian higher-up
4. Paulus rests here in Harmony
5. Athenian
6. What Yeats' falcon finds itself in
8. In the matter of
12. Place of rendezvous for Polly Peachum and Mack the Knife
13. Prospective hero or villain depending on whether you like Roe vs. Wade
14. Jud in *Oklahoma*
15. Something primitive, in Wallace Stevens
16. German philosopher, more optimistic than most

17. Is that in the *Syllabus*?
21. One of Michelangelo's finest
24. What Simple Simon did not have
26. The Medievals thought a day of this was no picnic
28. A rose, says he, is not always a rose
29. The Nightingale to close friends
30. Where it is

ACROSS:

2. A husband who got too far out ahead of his troops
7. A class of knights
9. Of little faith
10. Something in common between Bo and the tablets

11. Lost out to Lenin
13. According to Heidegger, it does the talking
15. It's eery above it
18. His initials, if someone had purloined his middle name
19. This theologian's always in process
20. A small word, but a big deal in Kierkegaard
22. Stevens had one, but he didn't give it to Sylvia
23. Every German city has a Haus for it
25. Sitcoms, planes, estate planning
26. Site of an early Murdoch novel
27. Disposition of the ladies who bested Sir John
29. *Till We Have. . .*
30. The way you talk, Zarathustra!
31. Exposed the wizard for Dorothy et al.

Soundings: An Interdisciplinary Journal
306 Aconda Court, University of Tennessee, Knoxville, Tennessee 37996-0530

Annual Subscription Rates: US individual $18; institution $27. Foreign individual $21, institution $30.

SPRING AUDIO

FREUD'S COCAINE PAPERS

by Art O Donoghue

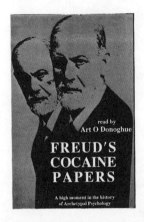

One Tape: 1 1/2 hrs $11.95

Robert Louis Stevenson used cocaine to beat writer's block (and then wrote *Dr. Jekyll and Mr. Hyde*), and President Grant used it to write his memoirs. These are a few of the tales in this account of Sigmund Freud's use of the drug and the events that led him to write the *Cocaine Papers*. Art O Donoghue and James Hillman rediscovered the *Papers* in Vienna and had them translated in 1963. In the tape's first part, Donoghue tells you all about it in a talk recorded at the now infamous Notre Dame Festival of Archetypal Psychology. In the second part, Donoghue reads excerpts from the *Papers* which show that their value is psychological and not pharmacological.

EROTIC POEMS OF THE EARL OF ROCHESTER

read by Ian Magilton

One Tape: 1 hr $11.95

The Earl of Rochester was Charles II's drinking pal and poet—bawdy, raucous, and yet elegant as only the rakes of the Restoration could be. The Puritans had been driven out at last, and there was a lot of lost time to make up. Rochester showed them how, with a wit that still rules after three hundred years. His poems were long suppressed (but smart schoolboys somehow always managed to find them!). English poetry would never be so erotic—or cool—again. The poems are read by Ian Magilton, the Obie-award winning actor of Roy Hart Theater fame.

ANALYTICAL PSYCHOLOGY SOCIETY

OF WESTERN NEW YORK

Program Announcement: Winter / Spring 1994

The listing below gives titles, as well as the presenters. Times and financial matters are included in the complete program, which is printed triannually.

THE ALCHEMY OF THE SOUL
a lecture by Ann Goldsmith

SOMATIZATION IN PRIVATE LIFE
a seminar with
Paul Kugler, Ph.D.

THE REDEMPTION OF AUTHENTIC LIFE
a lecture by
Catherine Johnson, M.S.W.

THE SYMBOLISM OF THE TREE
a workshop with
Catherine Johnson, M.S.W.

THE FOUR COUPLES WITHIN
a lecture by Robert Moore, Ph.D.

THE SACRED PROSTITUTE
A lecture and workshop by
Nancy Qualls-Corbett, Ph.D.

THE MAGIC DRUM
a lecture and workshop by
Beverly Bond Clarkson, M.A.
and Austin Clarkson, Ph.D.

ON DREAM WORK IN GROUPS
a lecture by
John Segmen, Ph.D.

The Analytical Psychology Society of Western New York, founded in 1976 as a not-for-profit, membership-supported organization, focuses on studies and concerns in analytic and archetypal psychology. Membership is open to the public; dues are tax-deductible. Benefits include reduced prices for books, workshops, classes, and lecture series.

For further information, write to: Analytical Psychology Society of Western New York • 375 Linwood Avenue • Buffalo NY 14209-1690 or call (716) 854-7457

SPRING PUBLICATIONS

Hell, The Underworld, Trauma, Darkness, Disease—and all their cousins

Greg Mogenson's *God Is a Trauma: Vicarious Religion and Soul-Making* brings religion and psychology together by presenting a theology of soul, rather than of the spirit. Faithfulness to the soul shifts our focus from the overwhelming nature of whatever functions as "God" to the small scale of daily soul-making. (167 pp., 0–88214–339–5)

Robert Bly writes of "The Age of Endarkenment" from *Letters at 3AM* that Michael Ventura "has written the greatest essay yet by a member of his generation." Andrei Codrescu says these essays "brilliantly diagnose our fin-de-siecle." Read this book to be "enlightened and enlivened" (Thomas Moore) about our collective psychic and political condition. (247 pp., 0–88214–361–1)

Impossible Love: Heresy of the Heart, by Jungian analyst Jan Bauer, addresses the vertical movement up into the heights and down into the Underworld of betrayal, taboos, and excess that characterizes tragic romances. The 12th-century passion between Heloïse and Abelard and a 20th-century woman's "relationship failures" provide case histories of these experiences that change lives forever. (204 pp., 0–88214–359–X)

Eugene Monick's *Evil, Sexuality, and Disease in Grünewald's Body of Christ* passionately attends to the sickly Christ on the cross of the Isenheim altarpiece. The (sexually?) diseased God-image offers compassionate relief to the burdens of personal guilt and shows the strange beauty shining through the disgust and unbearable pain of pandemic disease. Foreword by David L. Miller and color plates. (189 pp., 0–88214–356–5)